The Virtual
Management Office

Best Practices, Proven Methods

The Virtual Project Management Office

Best Practices, Proven Methods

Robert L. Gordon

Wanda Curlee

MANAGEMENTCONCEPTS

ʃʃʃ
MANAGEMENTCONCEPTS

8230 Leesburg Pike, Suite 800
Vienna, VA 22182
(703) 790-9595
Fax: (703) 790-1371
www.managementconcepts.com

Copyright © 2011 by Management Concepts, Inc.

Printed in the United States of America

Library of Congress Cataloging-in-Publication Data

Gordon, Robert L.
   The virtual project management office : best practices, proven methods/
Robert L. Gordon, Wanda Curlee.
      p. cm.
   ISBN 978-1-56726-327-5
1. Virtual reality in management. 2. Virtual work teams. 3. Project
management. I. Curlee, Wanda. II. Title.
HD30.2122.G67 2011
658.4'04—dc22

                                                    2011015841

10   9   8   7   6   5   4   3   2   1

ABOUT THE AUTHORS

Robert L. Gordon, DM, has been involved in managing virtual global projects for decades, managing dozens of dispersed teams and specializing in international procurement, contract management, supply chain practices, and logistical services. He develops and delivers courses for the American Public University System, the Keller Graduate School of Management (DeVry University), and the Apollo Group in operations management, distance education, business, ethics, critical thinking, economics, and project management. He has published numerous articles on project management, project complexity, supply chain management, strategic value-added purchasing, team conflict, virtual teams, and vendor relations.

Wanda Curlee, DM, PMP, PgMP, PMI-RMP, also a veteran of establishing and running virtual project management offices, tackles complex, international projects by bringing diverse parties together to attain shared goals. Currently a senior manager at a major consulting firm, Wanda is a program management leader experienced in global markets, government projects, and highly complex IT, information systems, and managed services projects. She is also an adjunct instructor for Northcentral University and Kaplan University, facilitating online doctoral, graduate, and undergraduate courses in project management, critical thinking, and strategic management. She is active on several PMI committees and has spoken at several congresses, specializing in program management, business continuity planning, team building and leadership, negotiations, and resourcing.

To my family, my rock of encouragement. My husband, Steve, is always standing by my side in every endeavor that I take, even when it means less time with him and more time in front of my laptop. My daughter, Tiffany, continues to inspire and refresh me, helping me see life through the eyes of a 16-year-old. Finally, to my sons, Paul and Sam: Thank you for your military service and for dedicating your lives to protecting our freedom.

—*Wanda Curlee*

To my late younger brother, William Paul Gordon. Although his life was cut short, William enjoyed a full life and made every moment special. He was always passionate about people. He always wanted to be around people and would make new friends quickly. William met people from all over the world, and he would often strike up conversations with strangers, just to learn about them and their lives. I dedicate this book to him because, with him and his affable nature in mind, I hope that each reader finds a new friend in the knowledge between these covers.

—*Robert Lee Gordon*

CONTENTS

PREFACE

Research has shown that an effective project management office (PMO) is a critical element in the success of an organization's projects—and, in turn, the organization itself. Yet PMOs have waxed and waned since the mid-1980s for various reasons. Project managers have had difficulty convincing business leaders that PMOs are meaningful and effective. Many senior leaders do not truly understand the full value of project management, let alone the PMO.

Times have changed. Technology and globalization have altered the traditional project management environment. Technology has allowed many projects to shift away from the office setting and has even encouraged businesses to conduct project management in a virtual environment. If project management is to survive as a discipline, the community must be flexible in incorporating technology, instituting flexible project environments, and continually developing new ways to measure a project's success.

PMO leaders often struggle with virtual projects because the requirements are so different. At the same time, project managers working on virtual projects will find that traditional project management offices do not usually provide the services needed in a virtual environment. Virtual project management offices—VPMOs—are designed to cater to the virtual project and the needs of the virtual project manager.

This book describes how VPMOs can successfully facilitate virtual work by providing tools that support the virtual environment and the organization as a whole. Virtual project management offices can offer new, more efficient services that create additional value for the organization.

Both experienced and novice PMO leaders will benefit from this book's guidelines and suggestions. It is arranged in four parts:

- Part I: PMOs and the Virtual Environment (Chapters 1–3)
- Part II: Soft Issues (Chapters 4–7)

- Part III: Best Practices (Chapters 8–10)
- Part IV: Policies, Programs, Training, and the Future (Chapters 11–14).

Chapters 1 through 3 discuss the background and history of project management offices and the virtual environment and offer guidance for getting started in implementing a VPMO. The second part, Chapters 4 through 7, addresses "soft" issues such as trust, organizational change, culture, and communication. Part III, Chapters 8 through 10, offers tools and templates and suggests best practices. The last section, Part IV, Chapters 11 through 14, provides handy hints on compliance with policies, procedures, and laws, as well as a discussion of program management and training and some final words.

For printable copies of the many surveys, checklists, workshop schedules, audit charts, assessments, and evaluations presented in the book and for other supplemental materials, go to www.managementconcepts.com/pubs and click on "Book Supplements," or contact Management Concepts at pubsupport@managementconcepts.com.

Robert L. Gordon

Wanda Curlee

May 2011

PMOs AND THE VIRTUAL ENVIRONMENT

Part I will help the reader understand the virtual project environment and how the virtual PMO (VPMO) can help the organization's leadership as well as the end user, the project manager.

Figure I-1 outlines the basics on virtual project management offices, which are covered in more detail in the following three chapters. These three chapters emphasize the importance of understanding the business case for creating a VPMO and implementing features that will benefit the company's particular environment. If the VPMO is to be successful, its leader and staff must understand what is important to the company's leadership and to the virtual project managers and other stakeholders.

Introduction to the Virtual Project Management Office
What Project Management Offices Do
Virtual Teams
Differences between Virtual Environments and Traditional Offices
The VPMO's Responsibilities

↓

The Need for a Virtual Project Management Office
Virtual Projects
Business Justifications and Drawbacks
Building a Business Case
Economic Justifications
Environmental Justifications
Marketing the VPMO

Establishing a Virtual Project Management Office
Organizational Structure
Planning the Implementation
Champion and Stakeholder Support
Metrics
Collaborating with Other Departments

Figure 1-1: The Virtual Project Management Office

Chapter 1

INTRODUCTION TO THE VIRTUAL PROJECT MANAGEMENT OFFICE

Before we delve deeper into our discussion of virtual project management offices, a discussion of project management offices in general is in order. There are many names for, and definitions of, the project management office (Hobbs and Aubry 2008), which can make determining whether to establish a project management office a confusing process. The Project Management Institute (PMI) gives a high-level definition of the term in *A Guide to the Project Management Body of Knowledge (PMBOK® Guide)* that may help clarify its meaning. According to PMI, a PMO is:

> An organizational body or entity assigned various responsibilities related to the centralized and coordinated management of those projects under its domain. The responsibilities of a PMO can range from providing project management support functions to actually being responsible for the direct management of a project. (Project Management Institute 2008, p. 435)

The project management office can be whatever it is defined to be—but this can be problematic. The PMO needs to offer value to project managers, of course, but it also needs to offer value all the way up the chain of command. The PMO leader must be careful, however, that the new PMO is not everything to everyone. Make sure that the systems in place, such as accounting systems, will support the metrics and activities promised by the new PMO. The quickest way for the PMO to fail is by not delivering on its promises. If the required systems are not in place at the beginning, the PMO will not be able to provide its intended support services and other deliverables.

WHAT PROJECT MANAGEMENT OFFICES DO

PMOs offer a number of benefits to the organization. They:

- Create standards for common processes and offer flexible templates, which saves the organization time and money; project managers do not have to build their own each time they start a project.

- Create and deploy new or revised processes and templates throughout the organization, facilitating organizational learning.

- Offer a data warehouse (manual or automated) of material that can be used by other project managers leading similar projects.

- Provide training to boost project managers' skills. This training is less expensive than that offered by outside contractors.

- Deliver project management coaching and intervention services to keep projects on track. If projects do fall behind, then the PMO will offer a risk management plan to correct the problems.

- Monitor universal data—standardized terminology, processes, procedures, and other information—on projects and advocate projects to internal and external stakeholders.

- Track project metrics organization-wide to keep everyone in the organization up-to-date.

- Advertise their project management services to individuals inside and outside the organization.

PMO Structures

PMOs can be classified as centralized, decentralized, or hybrid (combining the features of both centralized and decentralized PMOs). Research indicates that project managers do better with a centralized PMO (Curlee 2008). The centralized PMO is structured such that the project managers, project coordinators, and other personnel performing project activities report to an administrative chain of command within the PMO. The project personnel are assigned to projects by the administrative chain of command. The centralized PMO is responsible for PM training, PM organizational processes, and technology used and implemented by project managers. In addition, the PMO is responsible for evaluating project personnel's performance and compensation (Milosevic, Inman, and Ozbay 2001; Toney 2002).

Decentralized PMOs and hybrid PMOs appear to be more common (Hobbs and Aubry 2008). The decentralized PMO is normally responsible for maintaining PM methods, training, or both, as well as best practices. This type of PMO does not have a central decision-making authority. Authority may be delegated or collaborative (Ormand et al. 2000; Hales 1999; Kerzner 2009).

As noted, from a project manager's perspective, the centralized PMO provides the most support. From management's perspective, a decentralized or hybrid PMO is probably more cost-effective. There is no easy way to determine which kind will work best in a given organization. In general, the PMO needs to be planned carefully and must be able to flexibly respond to the organization's changes and needs.

PMO Types

At the macro level, there are three different types of project management offices: corporate, organizational, and the project/program PMO. Within these three macro levels, there are many variations.

The corporate PMO, sometimes called an enterprise PMO (EPMO), among other titles, normally reports to the executive level of leadership—perhaps the CEO, CIO, COO, or sometimes the CFO. The EPMO may also report to the head of a business unit. Depending on the organization's project management maturity, there may be several EPMOs, which may work independently of each other or may report to the one in the executive suite.

The EPMO, depending on leadership's need, will fit one of the PMO structures: centralized, decentralized, or hybrid. The designated PMO leader should create a business case and periodically update it to determine the structure of the PMO and whether the PMO is providing the correct tools, reports, and metrics for leadership and project managers.

The organizational PMO fits all the parameters of the EPMO (e.g., by providing metrics, reports, methodologies), but it is lower in the organization. An organizational PMO does not have the authority to make changes that affect the entire company. Any changes (assuming the PMO is allowed to make changes) would be made at the organizational level. These PMOs may work independently or may report to an EPMO. In a mature project management organization, it is likely that the organizational PMO would report to the EPMO, if it exists.

The last kind of PMO, the project management office that is established with each project, is the most common type and will not be discussed at length in this book. Depending on the size and length of the project, the PMO can be small or very large. It disbands at the end of the project.

Hurt and Thomas' (2009) study reported that senior management, project managers, and stakeholders found all types of project management offices beneficial and that they helped in the implementation of projects. Because of the benefits they offer, it is incumbent on PMO leaders to make sure that PMOs meet the needs of the organization and do not place undue demands—meaning extra work—on project managers.

VIRTUAL TEAMS

On a virtual project, more than 50 percent of the project team members are not resident in the same physical location, though they are not necessarily dispersed over different time zones. Team members depend on technology to communicate, rarely or never meet face-to-face more than once every two weeks, and are allowed to make decisions about the project (Kelley 2001; Townsend and DeMarie 1998; Maznevski and Chudoba 2000). (This definition is flexible; amend it to conform to your organization's needs as necessary.) Virtual projects may also be called *distributed projects, disbursed projects, remote projects, or telecommuting projects,* among other names. A similar nomenclature may be used for virtual project managers or team members.

Duarte and Snyder (2006, p. 5) identified seven types of virtual teams:

- Networked teams
- Parallel teams

- Project or product-development teams
- Work or production teams
- Service teams
- Management teams
- Action teams.

Networked teams and project teams are very similar in nature. Both cross geographic and organizational boundaries and time, and both have a common purpose. A project team maintains cohesiveness for a set period of time and performs non-routine tasks, whereas a networked team has no defined life span, and tasks are normally routine operations.

The virtual PMO deals with networked and project teams consistently. The PMO leader should work to enhance the communication of project teams with networked teams. When project managers understand networked teams' leaders and how networked teams work, they can help project teams succeed. Network teams are focused on a goal and individuals come and go (Duarte and Snyder 2006), which is remarkably similar to the way project teams work.

Virtual teams juggle more complexities than do traditional teams, including managing technology and crossing time, organizational, and geographical boundaries. Duarte and Snyder's (2006) studies indicate that the fluidity of the virtual team makes collaboration difficult: workflows may differ, cultures may clash, goals may vary, and technologies may be incompatible. Virtual project teams must be flexible enough to work on the edge of chaos or complexity when necessary.

Seven success factors must be present for these teams to be successful (Duarte and Snyder 2006). Technology is only one, as "virtual teams entail much more than technology and computers" (p. 9). The other six are:

- Human resource policies
- Training and on-the-job education and development
- Standard organizational and team processes
- Organizational culture
- Leadership support of virtual teams
- Team-leader and team-member competencies (pp. 12–13).

Virtual teams must also take legal issues into consideration. Depending on where the virtual project takes place, U.S. and foreign laws may apply. The U.S. laws may include state laws and federal laws such as the Racketeer Influenced and Corrupt Organizations Act (RICO) and the Foreign Corrupt Practices Act (FCPA). The PMO should institute training and understand how U.S. laws interact with applicable foreign laws.

DIFFERENCES BETWEEN VIRTUAL ENVIRONMENTS AND TRADITIONAL OFFICES

Virtual leadership requires a different skill set than does traditional face-to-face leadership. Trust is an integral aspect of virtual teams; without trust, a virtual team is more likely to fail (Cascio 2000; Kezsbom 2000). Executives dealing with virtual projects must ensure that people with the needed skills are in the right area when needed, must disseminate innovative best practices, and must identify talent throughout the organization. Specifically, the virtual PMO must ensure that the correct project managers are assigned to virtual projects.

Communication can present challenges in virtual environments. If English is the language of business, as it generally is, team members from different countries may not be native speakers, may use different words to mean the same thing, and may not understand regional nuances of the language. These concerns are mitigated in a traditional office. Body language clarifies spoken language and can help prevent misunderstandings. If written language is unclear, collocated project team members are able to clear up any misunderstandings almost immediately. In the virtual environment, this is not possible.

Boudreau and colleagues (1998) note that a virtual organization augments its chances of success by using a "federation concept"—in other words, by forming partnerships, joint ventures, consortia, and other creative alliances that change over time and with the needs of the virtual organization. This federation may include alliances with other internal organizations within the company or outside partners. This type of federation was successful for the B-1 Bomber project, which drew together more than 2,000 corporations, which interacted primarily virtually. Other successful corporations that employ the federation concept include Sun Microsystems, Nike, and Reebok.

A federation is unlikely to work in a traditional office that does not allow flexibility, does not have virtual projects, and depends on contractors and subcontractors to do major pieces of work. In a traditional office, management and leadership are always available to make decisions, the chain of command is fully functional, and management frowns if anyone attempts to subvert it. In a virtual environment, this is not true; the federated concept enhances decision-making.

The smooth integration of technology within the organization and among the federation members (Boudreau et al. 1998) allows local projects to have the support of a worldwide virtual organization. The client does not even realize that the product is the result of several companies or organizations working together. A well-run virtual organization should be able to function with very little regard to geographical distance and time barriers. In order to do so, the federated virtual environment must be technologically seamless, be responsive to local needs, and have the centralization necessary for efficiency. The virtual PMO will mediate this federated environment.

Additionally, a federated virtual organization must be flexible and responsive to the needs of the environment (Boudreau et al. 1998). Partnerships and alliances will disband as needed, and new alliances will be established depending on the needs of the project, the organization, or both.

By now, it should be evident that the virtual environment is different from the traditional project environment. Virtual project management offices must ensure that they provide the necessary tools and services to allow virtual project teams to succeed. There are many hidden traps awaiting the virtual project manager (e.g., a lack of standardized processes, tools, and templates), and the virtual PMO can alleviate many of them. When a virtual team does succeed, the organization's leadership must make a concerted effort to publicize its success throughout the organization (Duarte and Snyder 2006).

THE VPMO'S RESPONSIBILITIES

Virtual PMOs offer new savings to organizations by reducing organizational costs without sacrificing benefits to employees. They can be small or large organizations. Virtual project team members may report directly to the PMO, or the environment may be matrixed.

The VPMO establishes metrics, measures performance, and reports the results to a higher PMO, to the organization/corporation, or both. It must equip virtual teams with needed tools, systems, technology, templates, support, and methodology. The leadership of the VPMO must continually assess the effectiveness of these tools, systems, technology, templates, support, and methodology, as well as the demands being placed on the virtual project managers. VPMOs may provide some support to virtual project managers, preparing them to handle the unexpected.

The VPMO walks a tightrope. The VPMO staff must make sure to provide enough value to the virtual project manager because project managers supply information to the VPMO. If a project manager senses that he or she is not receiving quality service from the VPMO, he or she may start to provide spotty data to the VPMO, which in turn will undermine the credibility of the VPMO with the company's leadership. Sound complicated? That's because it is.

The VPMO leadership must adapt with the company's culture. An astute VPMO leader will understand how the virtual environment is changing and how the organization is accepting the virtual changes. The VPMO's processes, procedures, methodologies, technology, white papers, lessons learned, and templates should be updated to reflect these changes. At the same time, the VPMO staff should coordinate with other departments in the organization, such as legal and accounting, to update the same documents when relevant new regulations and legislation take effect.

Project management offices are a relatively new phenomenon in the world of project management. The virtual project management office is a newer adaptation still. As with all new phenomena, VPMOs need to find their place in the organization. Perhaps the biggest compliment that could be paid to a VPMO is that it is no longer needed because virtual project management has become a part of the culture of the organization. But in most organizations, VPMO leadership has a long way to go before this is true.

Before a VPMO can become an integral part of an organization's culture, the virtual organization must create a culture that is based on project management, starting with the top leadership and filtering down to project teams and those who support them. This will take three to five years at a minimum and can only occur when individuals from all organizational levels are committed to ensuring that the VPMO delivers virtual project management excellence.

Chapter 2

THE NEED FOR A VIRTUAL PROJECT MANAGEMENT OFFICE

When a company considers establishing a virtual project management office, the company's culture and the attitude of the company's leadership toward organizational change must be taken into account. The company must also consider practical matters, such as the number of projects it undertakes—particularly the number of virtual projects—and the number of project managers and project managers who work in remote settings. Companies with no virtual or distributed projects obviously have no need for a virtual project management office.

Other factors the company could consider might include:

- Offshore development
- Contractual requirements
- Location of clients (collocated or not)
- Location of subcontractors (collocated or not)
- Whether project personnel must travel to the project site
- Whether project personnel may work from other locations
- Whether the project is international, regional, or national in nature.

It is essential to develop a solid business case to support the establishment of a virtual project management office. This chapter details the elements that compose a business case and, more generally, will help you decide whether a VPMO is necessary and practical for your organization.

VIRTUAL PROJECTS

As described in Chapter 1, on a virtual project, the majority of virtual team members do not work in the same location. They rely on technology to communicate, have infrequent meetings, and are empowered to make project decisions. Individual organizations must establish the key factors that determine what makes a project virtual. The organization's leaders also need to determine whether virtual projects are an anomaly in the organization or an everyday occurrence. (If virtual projects are unusual in an organization, it might consider taking more on; they can increase the reach of the company and increase revenue.)

Virtual projects have existed since ancient times. Think of the pyramids of Egypt, the Incas and their elaborate road systems, and Solomon and his temple. Each of these project was completed with a project leader working in a remote location. The pharaoh was not on location when the pyramids were built. Solomon traveled extensively while the temple was being built. The Incan rulers ordering road construction didn't oversee progress in all its locations. In fact, the Incas built their roads starting on opposite ends, and much to archeologists' surprise, the roads met exactly in the middle.

So, how were those virtual projects different from today's? They differed in several important ways, the most significant of which is communication via technology. Today, technology allows for almost instantaneous communication worldwide, which facilitates virtual projects worldwide. The other differences are schedule and cost demands. Today, sponsors are worried about meeting a timetable and ensuring that projects meet their budgets (Curlee 2008).

Even though virtual projects are somewhat commonplace today, they are riddled with risk. Risk was not much of a consideration in ancient times. Resources were plentiful; schedule and costs were not an issue. Most project sponsors were dictators or tyrants, which allowed them to take total control over the project. In today's business world, law or culture prevents a single person from taking this kind of control.

BUSINESS JUSTIFICATIONS AND DRAWBACKS

There are several key business justifications for setting up a virtual project management office, but VPMOs also have some shortcomings, primarily in the area of communication. Business justifications include virtual teams' increased productivity; better access to global markets because virtual teams can cross national boundaries; fewer managers; and positive environmental impact, such as reduced automobile emissions (Cascio 2000; Elkins 2000). Shortcomings of VPMOs include the high cost to set up and maintain home offices for individual employees who telecommunicate and communication challenges, including workers' feelings of isolation from others in the organization (Cascio 2000).

IBM has conducted internal studies of virtual employees' productivity and has found that productivity increased between 15 percent and 40 percent for virtual employees, compared with typical office employees. Productivity increases in customer service have also been documented. Arthur Anderson cites an increase of 25 percent in direct contact with customers for sales personnel working virtually (Cascio 2000). Cascio (2000) has also documented problem-solving productivity gains for people working virtually.

Virtual project management organizations allow groups more effective access to global markets. Since virtual organizations can transverse national boundaries via email, phone calls, collaborative software, and other online tools, individuals no longer have to be present on-site to be effective. Major organizations have used virtual design and engineering teams to develop projects without requiring all of the design work to be done face-to-face (Cascio 2000). Major projects are also commonly completed virtually, and in many cases these projects are completed without people ever having met face-to-face. Virtual teams have enhanced global competitiveness for all types of project teams.

In virtual project management organizations, leadership shifts according to the requirements or objectives of the organization (Lipnack and Stamps 1997). Virtual organizations require fewer managers because they make use of shared leadership: every individual is required to take some leadership role, even if only for a short while. Shared leadership improves effectiveness while reducing the need for management overseers.

Telecommuting leads to another important benefit of virtual organizations: a reduction in automobile emissions. If more companies made more of their work virtual, vehicle emissions would drop dramatically. In an example from Georgia Power, 150 telecommuters reduced automobile emissions by 35,000 pounds annually (Cascio 2000). If this example is scaled up, the environmental impact is dramatic. If 100 million U.S. workers were to telecommute, the reduction in emissions would be over 23 billion pounds of emissions across the United States. The opportunity to reduce emissions on such a scale can have a significant environmental impact. Needless to say, the virtual project management organization is a very green organization. Reducing workers' need to commute to a central office location also will lead to changes in the landscape—fewer skyscrapers will be built, and there will be less traffic, making for a quieter world (Handy 1995).

On the negative side, setting up and maintaining a virtual office is not free. The initial capital investment ranges from $3,000 to $8,000, and annual upkeep will cost about $2,000 (Lai and Burchell 2008). The virtual organization also must invest in technology. Virtual team members must all have access to electronic tools such as email, an instant messenger program, and collaborative technologies such as Net Meeting© and Groove™. Many of these programs are or can be free, but virtual organizations usually provide people with laptops—which would add to the cost of setting up a VPMO.

BUILDING A BUSINESS CASE

An organization's culture, risk tolerance, assessment of its bottom line, and need for future revenue may drive the company's leadership to consider taking on virtual projects or striving to understand virtual projects better by creating a virtual project management office. Some organizations jump straight into implementing a VPMO without establishing a business case for it, but developing a business case is the commonsense and most practical business-sense way to determine whether a virtual project management office is needed. The PMO leader, the business unit leaders, and the PMO sponsor should all partner to develop the business case, which helps ensure that all parties within the organization understand the pros and cons of establishing a VPMO.

The business case analyzes the "whys" of creating a VPMO. Assuming the company has or will have a virtual project community, how would a virtual PMO help the virtual teams *and* the company's leadership—the PMO's two masters? Keep in mind that any PMO must not only benefit project teams and company leaders; it must also help the organization/corporation in general.

The first step in building a business case should be a requirements analysis. This should be a gap analysis—in other words, a study of where the organization is and where it needs to be. The PMO leader and staff members collect requirements from the leadership, sponsor, project managers, end users, stakeholders, and any other pertinent sources. From this list, the PMO leaders can start to develop a business case.

The business case should address the topics listed below. In addition to these, the team writing the business case should consider in its standard business case template other factors that are important to the company or organization or in the industry.

- Determine success factors
  - What will determine the VPMO's success in the organization?
  - Ensure the success factors are measurable (often, accounting systems cannot measure project metrics).
  - Ensure that the success factors are important to leadership.
  - When will these success factors be measured?
  - Remember, the VPMO's disappearance—its becoming an integrated part of the organization—may be the best success factor of all!

- Analyze requirements
  - Technology (hardware/software)
    - Will the VPMO be responsible for project management hardware and software?
    - If not, will the VPMO have any influence?
    - Will the VPMO have any influence on accounting software?
    - Will the VPMO be responsible for group/collaboration software?
    - If not, will the VPMO have any influence on group/ collaboration software?

- Organization (corporate/business)
  - Where will the VPMO be organizationally?

○ Remember that a corporate VPMO and a business VPMO may function very differently. A corporate VPMO may have business VPMOs reporting to it or may work independently. It reviews projects/programs at a strategic level while business VPMOs normally review projects/programs at a tactical level.

○ What influence will the VPMO have on project managers and decision-making within projects?

○ Will portfolio management be one of the VPMO's functions?

- Implementation

  ○ How will the VPMO be implemented: will there be a big bang, slow rollout, or something in between? Take into account the company's culture.

  ○ What is the company's appetite for organizational change? How much change has the company gone through recently?

  ○ Make sure the project managers are involved in the implementation.

- Training

  ○ With major organizational changes, training must be a part of the implementation.

  ○ Will project management training be the responsibility of the VPMO?

  ○ Will training be conducted in conjunction with the training department? Who will maintain the budget? Who will have the overriding authority?

  ○ Determine if current training is adequate for virtual projects.

  ○ Determine if one-off training for virtual projects will be a responsibility of the VPMO.

- Reporting/metrics

  ○ Consider the project maturity of the organization.

  ○ Consider the accounting tools and what metrics can be automated.

  ○ Consider the metrics that are important to leadership.

○ Consider what data can be given back to the project managers in the field.

- Policies/procedures/processes
  ○ Determine which policies/procedures/processes will be under the ownership of the VPMO.
  ○ Determine which corporate and organizational policies/procedures/processes need to be adapted for virtual projects.
  ○ Determine ownership of the project management methodology. Will the VPMO ensure the project management methodology is adapted for virtual aspects of projects?
  ○ Will the VPMO update the project teams on new laws, lessons learned, and other virtual aspects (e.g., technology, updated processes and procedures, groupware)?

- Analyze gaps
  ○ Consolidate reporting and metrics
    - Once decisions are made regarding reporting, metrics, and tools, plans must be made to close the gaps between the current state and the future state.
  ○ More effective reporting and metrics
    - Determine the tool set to be used in the future.
  ○ Technology
    - Establish a budget that will meet the needs of the new VPMO.
    - Does the VPMO determine its own technology needs?
    - Does the VPMO rely on the IT budget for project management technology?

Ensure that subject matter experts—in other words, project managers—are asked their opinion about the business case. The best way to get project managers' buy-in to the new VPMO is to involve them so that they are a part of the process.

ECONOMIC JUSTIFICATIONS

Technology has made it easy for even the smallest business to connect to the global economy. In theory, a company just needs to post a site on the Internet to become a global business. Technology has also facilitated virtual projects. Virtual projects are considered essential in many large companies, such as those in the consulting industry. Many large companies have satellite locations. When these companies implement enterprise solutions or solutions for clients that are not located near the company's headquarters, then a company relies on a combination of local resources and resources from headquarters. The resources do not normally collocate; this would be prohibitively expensive.

A virtual PMO would help coordinate these virtual projects and monitor them. Depending on the responsibilities outlined in the VPMO's charter, it might staff the projects, develop staff projections, structure the projects into programs and portfolios, ensure that processes and procedures meet the needs of the virtual projects, train virtual project teams in applicable laws and culture, and monitor the processes, policies, and procedures for the virtual aspects of projects. The VPMO would centralize the administrative and tactical aspects of the virtual projects. Normally, this is economically advantageous to the organization (Hobbs and Aubry 2008).

ENVIRONMENTAL JUSTIFICATIONS

The virtual environment is in constant flux. Virtual projects are complex simply because they are distributed. In the Western business world, people have come to expect change within their organizations because of the prevalence of flat organizations, downsizing, and matrix structures. Downsizing has led to fewer individuals in the organizations, which has led to more matrix management and a shorter chain of command. These factors drive the environmental reasons for building a VPMO. According to the Project Management Institute's *PMBOK® Guide*, environmental factors can be external or internal elements "that surround or influence [a] project's success" (Project Management Institute 2008, p. 14).

When defining the role of the VPMO, its leadership must understand that the VPMO will face a number of factors that will affect projects but that it cannot control. Because environmental factors are continually changing, VPMO leaders may have to deal with significant volatility depending on the industry. Because of the likelihood of environmental change, VPMO leadership and staff need to ensure that processes and procedures are in place to update the methodology, training, management plans, and any policies that will affect virtual projects. Environmental factors that should be monitored may include the following:

- International and domestic laws
- Organizational changes
- Trends within the industry
- Court decisions within the industry
- How the company is perceived within the marketplace
- How the company is perceived internationally
- How the company is perceived in each country where there is a virtual project.

Let's say that a company realizes that a court ruling will affect it negatively whether the court case is won or not (the court case is not against the company). Regardless of the outcome, the company will be forced to change many policies, procedures, and modes of doing work. The VPMO will have to analyze how the new requirements will affect project managers in the field and working internationally.

MARKETING THE VPMO

The success of a VPMO depends in part on buy-in up and down the chain of command. The VPMO must provide value to senior managers as well as project managers, and people at all levels of the organization should tout its benefits. If a VPMO does not actually help people or its stakeholders do not promote its benefits, it is more likely to fail.

Project managers can market the value of the VPMO through pilot projects and then demonstrate them through lessons learned. What are some other ways that VPMO staff can demonstrate the worth of the VPMO? By providing proactive training; not simply being "yes people"; understanding and meeting project managers' needs and some of their wants; and meeting the needs of the leadership. The staff needs to ensure that new policies and procedures and updates to the organization's project management methodology always have project managers' buy-in. (Remember that buy-in does not necessarily equal acceptance.)

Virtual project management offices are not right for all companies. If a company does not have any virtual projects, a VPMO is not necessary. To truly understand the needs of the company or the organization and determine whether a VPMO is needed, an unbiased business case is a necessity.

The business case will reveal, to those doing the analysis as well as leadership, if there is a real need for a VPMO (or if it is just a whim of a few people in the organization) and, if so, what the VPMO must be and do. When possible, ask individuals who do not believe a VPMO is needed to review the business case. Their input will force the VPMO's proponents to make the business case stronger and will prepare them for presenting the business case to leadership, who may not immediately accept the concept.

VPMOs have general economic and environmental benefits. They can help companies save money by coordinating remote project work, which allows them to avoid expensive collocation efforts, and they can help organizations manage rapid or frequent organizational change.

Even if there are many good reasons for an organization to form a VPMO, the VPMO may not succeed if it doesn't help people at all levels of the organization and if people do not tout its benefits.

Chapter 3

ESTABLISHING A VIRTUAL PROJECT MANAGEMENT OFFICE

Once the business case has been approved, the hard work of setting up the virtual PMO begins. The new leadership of the VPMO must understand what the VPMO is to be and do and must develop an implementation strategy. This chapter will guide the reader through establishing a VPMO at the corporate level, though the same advice applies to establishing a VPMO at any level of a company.

The new VPMO leaders probably have a lot on their minds and are feeling overwhelmed. The new endeavor must be viewed as a project and run as a project, which will help everyone involved understand its goals. The leaders should begin by holding a kickoff meeting with all involved parties, especially the sponsor, to ensure that nothing has changed since the business case was approved, assign and clarify roles and responsibilities, ensure business leaders understand the VPMO's role, and so forth.

Also at the outset, leaders should strive to determine the type of organizational change management process that the VPMO will require. Organizational change management may be minimal for a standalone VPMO, but a VPMO that extends throughout the corporation or organization may require an extensive organizational change management program (see Chapter 5 for more information on change management).

ORGANIZATIONAL STRUCTURE

A corporate VPMO may be standalone or organizational. The existence of a standalone VPMO does not necessarily mean that there aren't other PMOs in the company. The other PMOs will not officially interact with the corporate VPMO or with any of the other PMOs. In fact, the PMO leaders may not know the others exist. This structure can be counterproductive for the project manager and ultimately for leadership.

A corporate VPMO, whether it has authority over other organizational PMOs or not, must have knowledge of the other PMOs. This allows for collaboration and sharing of lessons learned and ensures that the project managers are not made to do duplicative "stuff" for the various PMOs and VPMOs. The corporate VPMO can also keep the executive suite informed about organizational activities while the other PMOs can keep their own leadership informed about what their counterparts and corporate are doing. If the corporate VPMO has no knowledge of the other PMOs, project managers will likely become disillusioned with the lack of cooperation between the various PMOs. Eventually, the VPMO and PMOs may collaborate or set up a reporting structure. The project managers ultimately benefit when PMOs collaborate.

If the corporate VPMO is organizational, all of the other PMOs in the company report to it. This dynamic benefits project managers because it promotes collaboration. Organizational VPMOs should also drive more consistency within the company. Lessons learned can be quickly disseminated and implemented among the PMOs.

No matter what organizational structure is chosen, the VPMO leadership must ensure that the VPMO organization meets their needs as well as those of the project managers. This will minimize any risks and increase constituents' acceptance of the VPMO.

PLANNING THE IMPLEMENTATION

The VPMO leadership needs to approach the implementation of the VPMO as a project. The project must start with an approved business case and follow all of the best practices of project management. Figure 3-1 shows a sample work breakdown structure (WBS) for establishing a VPMO. This WBS is notional and high-level; it can be used as a starting point for a company considering a VPMO.

Today, many companies have their own project management methodologies. The staff that is implementing the VPMO would

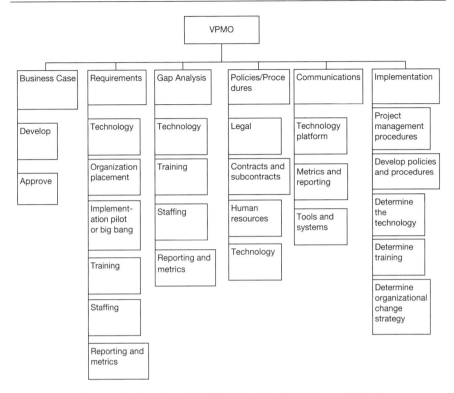

Figure 3-1:   Sample WBS for Establishing a VPMO

be encouraged to use company templates, which will help them become intimately familiar with the company's methodology. In turn, they can determine how the methodology can be adapted for project managers in the field. Tools that the project manager uses also should be used by the staff while implementing the VPMO. Working with the templates and tools will show the staff and leadership how the methodologies, tools, and corporate systems interact with each other.

Figure 3-2 shows a notional rollout plan that begins after the business case is approved. The predecessor numbers given in the schedule represent the tasks or subtasks that have to occur before another task or subtask can begin. The schedule does not set timeframes and is not resource-loaded because timing and resources are very dependent on circumstance and the organization or company.

Task Number	Summary Tasks	Tasks	Subtasks	Predecessor
1	Project Management			
2		Develop schedule		
3		Develop project plans		
4			Develop risk management plan	
5			Develop project plan	
6			Develop test plan	
7			Develop financial plan	
8			Develop communication plan	
9			Develop training plan	
10		Maintain schedule		2, 5
11		Status meetings		
12		Risk meetings		4
13		Determine project team		
14		Determine project tools		
15		Determine success criteria		
16		Determine monthly budget		2, 5, 7

Task Number	Summary Tasks	Tasks	Subtasks	Predecessor
17		Determine resource plan		5, 13
18		Establish project management information system		
19	Policies/ Procedures			
20		Review policies affecting virtual projects		3
21		Coordinate with legal department		3
22		Coordinate with human resources		17
23		Determine the countries where projects are active		2, 3
24		Start crafting new policy and procedures as needed		20, 21, 22
25			Review process	24
26			Approval	25
27		Amend existing policy and procedures as needed		24, 25, 26
28			Review process	27
29			Approval	28

Task Number	Summary Tasks	Tasks	Subtasks	Predecessor
30		Amend existing project management methodology for virtual projects		26, 29
31			Review process	30
32			Approval	31
33	**Metrics**			
34		Determine what will be measured now		5, 6, 14, 15
35		Determine what will be measured at a later date		5, 6, 14, 15, 34
36		Determine manner in which metrics will be collected		24, 35
37		Determine manner in which metrics will be reported		8, 24, 36
38		Determine any gaps		35
39		Develop a contingency for the gaps		4, 38
40	**Technology**			
41		Who owns project management tools?		5, 24, 27

Task Number	Summary Tasks	Tasks	Subtasks	Predecessor
42		Determine the tool set for virtual projects		18
43		Automate methodology, tool sets, templates		18, 42
44		Work with IT to implement methodology for virtual projects		18, 42, 43

Figure 3-2:   A Sample Rollout Plan for a VPMO

Best practice: Consider the timeline and people involved with the implementation of a VPMO. Make sure to take into account organizational politics, which can slow or impede progress toward building a successful VPMO.

CHAMPION AND STAKEHOLDER SUPPORT

Successful PMOs are those that have leadership's support. VPMOs are no different. Organizational champions "that are committed, persistent, and courageous in advocating innovation" enhance any PMO's ability to succeed (Bass 1990, p. 219). A VPMO champion must be a forward-looking and progressive-thinking leader who understands the complexities involved with establishing something new or altering something that is established (such as an existing PMO). The VPMO champion should be well respected, provide real leadership, and have the authority needed to develop the new team.

The VPMO assigns a senior executive to the position of VPMO champion, and that person then helps the VPMO staff navigate the politics of the organization, pick and choose their battles, and structure presentations in a manner appropriate for particular leaders. He or she will grease the skids during the business case process, will influence individuals during implementation, and will be a mentor/advocate and feedback loop to ensure the VPMO continues to thrive and provide a valuable service to its stakeholders.

> **Best practice:** The VPMO needs a supportive sponsor who will drive the establishment of the VPMO. It is easy to become discouraged during this challenging process, so it is best to make sure that leadership is behind the process.

Rallying the Stakeholders around the Implementation

Virtual project management cannot be done in silence. The VPMO should have a communications plan from the outset. To start, the implementation of the VPMO is (in most cases) an organizational change that should be communicated throughout the organization. The organization's most senior leaders should announce the creation of the VPMO, usually through an email blast. The message should be brief; it should simply say that a VPMO is about to launch and explain what the VPMO will do.

Subsequent messages should be short, periodic updates; these might appear in a company newsletter or on the company's intranet site. Occasionally, there may be a feature on someone working on virtual projects, but the crux of each message should be what the VPMO will do for the stakeholders. It is recommended that each update focus on a different group of stakeholders.

As the launch comes closer, the leadership may send weekly or daily messages until the organization goes live. Following go-live, the VPMO may want to interview certain stakeholders and publish success stories. As the VPMO becomes integrated into the organization, the staff must make sure that all stakeholders remember that the VPMO exists. There are various ways the VPMO can communicate with stakeholders: continue to publish periodic newsletter updates, feature a stakeholder in the newsletter, feature a project in the newsletter, do a lunch and learn for the organization, or a segment of the organization, and organize lessons-learned discussion sessions for virtual project managers.

Best practices: As a project is coming due, make sure to send daily messages, as defined by the communications plan, about its arrival. A new project should be just as anticipated as the arrival of a new baby.

Meeting Organizational and Individual Needs

A VPMO demands additional overhead from project managers if it is to meet the requirements of the VPMO's leadership, but too much overhead will kill the VPMO. Why? Generally, project managers are very busy. They will only tolerate so many additional requirements before they hesitate or conveniently forget to provide information to the PMO. This is not done out of maliciousness—it is a matter of survival. Most project managers have enough to do in the field without, for example, having to complete extra reports for the VPMO. The leadership and staff of the VPMO must realize that without the support of the project managers in the field, the PMO will not succeed.

At the same time, the VPMO must meet the requirements of its sponsors, who will want results. Results come in various forms, but they ultimately depend on information that comes directly or indirectly from project managers. Some data will be extracted from the accounting system and centralized project management databases. Other reports may come from existing data already created by project managers. Whenever possible, the VPMO *staff* should create reports from data it extracts from various sources. Refrain from asking project managers to create new reports for the convenience of the VPMO.

The VPMO leaders and staff must carefully craft the implementation of the VPMO, including what processes and procedures will be changed and what the project managers will need as a result of those changes; what training project managers and leadership will need; when changes must be made; and how much say the VPMO will have over accounting systems, project management systems, and other tools that affect the virtual aspects of projects. These include group share software, email systems, social networking sites (such as Facebook and LinkedIn), and instant messaging. Virtual systems are essential to the virtual project manager and the team and can even be a matter of safety for projects taking place in hostile locations. A communications plan is essential and may be based on redundant communication systems to ensure the safety of project team members.

The staff and leaders must also determine how to keep the VPMO current and flexible to meet the demands of leadership and, most importantly, those of the project managers. Remember that project managers are the ones who bring in the revenue. The VPMO and the company's leadership's goals, whether stated or not, should focus on making the lives of virtual project managers as easy as possible so that they can better meet clients' demands. Keep in mind that virtual projects are already more difficult than traditional projects. There are more lines of communication, and there is no or little face-to-face communication. This makes a relatively simple project complex and a complex project quite difficult.

METRICS

The metrics that the VPMO will use should have been outlined in detail in the business case. The business case should answer the following questions, which will drive the initial metrics.

- What will be measured?
- What is important to leadership?
- What will help the virtual project manager?
- What will increase project management maturity?

Certain factors related to metrics must also be taken into consideration. For example, what type of accounting system does the company currently have? Will the accounting system support traditional project accounting, such as earned value management (EVM)? If not, how will the VPMO team handle EVM? Will the VPMO ask that the accounting system be altered to handle EVM? Does leadership support these changes? If so, is a project team in place to handle the changes to the accounting system while the VPMO is being implemented? Does doing it this way make sense? Remember to evaluate the availability of resources and determine a logical approach that fits the maturity of the organization.

In addition to the metrics covered in the business case, the VPMO should consider using others that the accounting system can readily provide and that are already familiar to the leadership and project managers. Metrics that are fairly easy to implement include cash flow, burn rate, return on investment, days sales outstanding, and accounts receivable. Other metrics outside EVMS, accounting, and financials may also be useful (e.g., customer surveys).

Issues tracking, software defect tracking (for software implementations), and risk tracking also should all be part of the initial metrics. The VPMO must determine the level at which these should be measured. It is common to look for and analyze trends in issues, defects, and risks in the virtual environment.

The VPMO may consider developing estimation tools specifically geared towards virtual projects. Many people do not understand that virtual projects may demand extra resources and do demand more of the project manager's time. Virtual project managers must make extra efforts to stay in touch with their teams—to hold team members accountable and responsible for keeping on schedule and keeping others informed and to assess the health of the team—as well as that of the project sponsor and stakeholders.

The project manager *must* develop a schedule within a schedule just for the virtual aspects of projects to mitigate the particular risks of virtual work (Mayer 2010). When estimating project schedules, the VPMO should build in extra time for developing the schedule within a schedule and should consider having a template for it. The schedule within a schedule should include tasks the project manager must complete, such as making sure to call or otherwise contact team leads (or, on a small project, everyone) at least weekly. These weekly calls should not be about work status; they should be more informal calls to really connect with the person. The schedule within a schedule should include time for dealing with individual accountability; efforts to make sure team members do not feel too isolated; conference calls with the project team; project publicity; celebrations; and other efforts to make up for the lack of face-to-face communication (e.g., by using webcams to see people, posting photos, using groupware).

> **Best practice:** There must be a schedule within a schedule to keep the project moving forward. Be sure to share the schedule within a schedule with team members, the sponsor, and other stakeholders, to help explain the importance of viewing the virtual aspect of the project as a process in itself.

In a virtual environment, it may not be possible to pick up the phone or run down the hall to ask someone for the latest configuration of a document or for the latest requirements. That's part of the reason why it is difficult to keep configuration control of documents and requirements on a virtual project. It may be especially challenging if there are no standards set for configuration tools or, even more fundamental, if there are no policies or procedures governing configuration. By establishing metrics around requirements and configuration, the VPMO can push for standardization and, over time, for relevant tools. The metrics should demonstrate the need for standardization if none exists; the project managers will demand tools if there is a requirement for standardization. Project managers will want standardization because it will facilitate the execution of their projects, and they want appropriate tools to help them achieve standardization.

Last but certainly not least, the VPMO must determine whether it will offer portfolio management. It is recommended that this not be an initial offering. Before it can take on portfolio management, the VPMO needs to look at how projects are grouped and how they could be grouped. Perhaps certain industries already group together within the company, but gathering data is difficult because of the way the systems work; alternatively, maybe it would make sense to group particular projects, but the company captures data for different groups in entirely different ways. Gathering statistics and data and performing trend analysis can help VPMOs determine whether there is an appetite for portfolio analysis (usually there is) for virtual projects and the best manner to present the data that will be used in portfolio management.

COLLABORATING WITH OTHER DEPARTMENTS

The VPMO staff should be the center of coordination with the rest of the organization's internal services, such as human resources, legal, finance, contracts, subcontracts (vendor management), IT, and more. Each of these internal groups has something that is needed for virtual projects. What can the VPMO do with each to help the corporation streamline the virtual aspects of projects or help virtual project managers? (Keep in mind that the VPMO will constantly be asked to justify its existence.)

In coordination with the human resource department, the VPMO may develop training and policies and procedures and modify the methodology for hiring and firing project personnel in various countries. The legal department can provide updates on any new or impending legislation that may affect the industry in which your company operates or that may affect project managers in remote locations. It can explain how to determine the laws in foreign countries and what to do when U.S. laws and other countries' laws conflict. You may want to ask the legal department for updates to the Foreign Corrupt Practices Act, the Sarbanes-Oxley Act, or any other laws or statutes that project managers and their teams need to know about.

The financial department should be closely tied to the VPMO. Many of the metrics the VPMO uses should come from the existing accounting system(s). VPMO staff should find out whether the accounting systems are project-based, or if the project manager or VPMO staff have to manipulate the data from these systems to determine the financials for a project. The VPMO can advocate for project management by requesting tools for project budgeting. Can modules be added to the system to allow for project accounting? Can the company start small by changing its timekeeping practices to suit projects? The VPMO should constantly work with the finance department to advocate for project-based finance. Remember to keep financial training for the VPMO staff up-to-date.

Contracts and subcontracts are sometimes handled by one department, but larger organizations handle contracts and subcontracts separately. Work with the applicable departments to see if a template can be developed that would allow the virtual project manager to manage a contract or subcontract to a certain point. Also, work with the contract department(s) to create standard nondisclosure statements.

Because some contracts and subcontracts may work in foreign countries, the legal department may be involved as well. Make sure the VPMO has established policies and procedures for work in as many countries as possible. If a project starts in a new country, the VPMO should help the project manager learn about the country's culture, laws, and other topics that may affect the project.

The VPMO staff needs to work with the IT department to determine the availability of tools, their cost, and the budget required for implementation of new tools. The VPMO would then need to work on a business case for tools, including a suite of project management tools, to enhance the quality of virtual projects.

In short, the VPMO needs to be the advocate for the virtual project manager. There needs to be a feedback loop between the VPMO and project managers on what is and what is not working in the field. When at all possible, the VPMO should push to automate as much as possible for the project teams. Project management tools for new projects should feature:

- Content-rich templates. The VPMO staff should complete common templates with common information. For example, it might provide five to ten content-rich templates for a risk management plan; each template would be intended for a different industry, sector, or product.

- Automatic completion of header information on documents.

- A built-in workflow that simplifies communication and the approval process, ensures that documents go to the correct people for approval, and is easily adapted by the project manager.

Implementing a VPMO is difficult and daunting. Some would argue that once the business case is approved, the implementation should be easy because the leadership's approval and sponsorship has been won. In reality, implementation can be a tricky sequence of events. If it is not done in a fashion that is logical for the company, and if the VPMO does not bring value to both the virtual project manager and the leadership, the VPMO is likely to fail.

The astute VPMO leader will understand the organizational culture of the company or organization, its project management maturity, and its tolerance of new project management concepts. It is a best practice to take a close look at the organization and determine how far along it is toward being ready for a virtual project management office. Consider its stage of maturity and what can be done to move it further along.

The astute VPMO leader will have the endorsement of several strong, well-respected, and senior project managers. When possible, these individuals should serve in various roles; they might act as the implementation lead, stakeholders, part of the executive committee, or subject matter experts. Project managers will be needed to help define the metrics, policies and procedures, systems, and training that are unique to the virtual project environment. New ideas, metrics, policies and procedures, tools, and methods should be presented in a manner that virtual project managers will readily accept.

A VPMO is, in short, the project manager's advocate. It can offer project managers and other stakeholders the best level of service—and prove its worth—by collaborating with other departments in the company, including human resources, legal, finance, contracts, subcontracts (vendor management), and IT.

PART II

SOFT ISSUES

Trust, change, culture and communication—known as soft issues—can make or break a virtual project. Figure II-1 offers a map of the soft issues that are significant in a VPMO and which the VPMO should address. The VPMO needs to ensure the project manager and the team members are equipped to foster and increase trust and understand how to cope with change. It must provide training aligned with the organization's culture as well as training in working with diverse people in a virtual environment. It must also develop a schedule to ensure that the project manager maintains active communication with the project team members.

Trust
Building Trust
The Pillars of Trust
Assessing Trust
Managing Politics
Trust Pitfalls

↓

Change
Responding to Change
Coping with Change
Supporting Change
Branding Change
Delegating Change

Culture
Understanding Culture
Attributes of Culture
Coping with Dysfunctional Culture
Changing Culture
Creating a Flexible Culture
Balancing Different Needs

↓

Communication
Special Considerations in a VPMO
Challenges
Communicating with Stakeholders
Organizational Structure and Communication
Coping with Negative Communication
Delivering Clear, Direct, and Cross-cultural Information
Delegating and Relegating Communication
Sources of Risk
Elements of Communication

Figure II-1:   Building a Virtual Project Management Office

Chapter 4

TRUST

As organizations, nations, and statesmen fail in the eyes of the public, trust has become a scarce commodity in society. Now more than ever, big business is a target of social distrust. However, organizational trust should actually be high on the priority list of any company that wants to be around in the future. Too many organizations ignore the importance of engendering trust and then find themselves in trouble later. A VPMO must understand how to build organizational trust in order to keep the organization vibrant and healthy.

Trust is difficult to create within a virtual organization because there are several factors already working against it. The problem with creating virtual trust is two-fold. The first problem, which exists in any organization (including a VPMO), is that people have a need to create separation between themselves and others. The second is that the more virtual the organization, the less communication there is between individuals, so trust is harder to build.

The first obstacle to building trust is an inherent part of being human, so it will be a continual struggle. People intrinsically want to be held apart from others—but they do not want to be alone. They want to feel as if they are part of a group, which can be defined internally or externally. It is easiest to define a group by external forces. The moment there is a visible separation between people—the moment they can claim "my nation," "my state," "my city," "my neighborhood"—the concept of a group exists. With this separation comes the concept of the "other," which is a barrier to trust because it creates a division that must be overcome.

Trust is an integral part of a successful virtual team (Anderson et al. 1998; Duarte and Snyder 2006; Lipnack and Stamps 1997; Handy 1995). But building trust in this kind of organization can be more difficult than in a traditional organization. Within a virtual organization, one challenge to building trust is that the organization will create its own boundaries based on prior project teams or functional areas, which can create rifts within the organization. The virtual project management office must then create commonalities between people to mitigate any internal divisions. But if the natural reaction is to distrust those who are separate from us, how can people who are not collocated come together? How can the VPMO create a feeling of trust between people who may have little connection with one another? On top of the challenges inherent in building trust between people who work in disparate locations and who may barely know one another, virtual team membership may be fluid and short-lived.

The project manager must be the one to draw together the project group in a way that builds community. To create and maintain trust, the leader of a virtual team should establish, maintain, and evolve consistent values and boundaries. Respect for others is an essential part of building trust. It's particularly important for supervisors in a virtual environment to trust and respect virtual employees (Anderson et al. 1998). Supervisors can create a sense of trust and respect by keeping their word; holding individuals accountable; establishing an ethical standard, living by it, and ensuring that project members live by it as well; and being a dependable source of support for the team at any time. Here are some initiatives that can help build community in a group, which in turn generates trust:

- Team newsletters
- Logo wear to celebrate a specific project
- Stakeholder meetings
- Celebrations of team successes
- Recognition of team and individual efforts.

> **Best practice:** Make trust part of the daily agenda. When you delegate a task, make sure to let the person to whom you are giving the work know that you trust him to get the job done.

The single greatest factor in building trust is team success. If a project is successful, trust suddenly materializes. Suddenly everything is golden and good, and team differences fade into the background. If project success is the panacea for trust, then project failure is its nemesis. Project failure will torpedo any efforts to build trust faster than any other factor. The moment a project starts to falter, the faster people will try to distance themselves from the project (or organization) in order to avoid being associated with the failure, because project failure is associated with personal failure.

> **Best practice:** Holding people accountable for producing good work will improve quality, increase the team's chances of success—and build even more trust.

BUILDING TRUST

The challenge is to build trust over time, which will help to create a reserve of trust. This reserve is very important for creating long-term trust, but it is also very difficult to achieve. So where does this advice leave the project manager who is worried about trust? The best way to find out if there is trust in an organization is to ask. Give all of the project stakeholders a quick, anonymous survey, as shown in Figure 4-1.

Project Trust Survey	*Yes*	*No*
Do you trust your organization?		
Do you trust your team?		
Do you trust your coworkers?		
Do you trust your boss?		
Do you trust your boss's boss?		

Figure 4-1: Trust Survey

This simple survey can give the virtual project manager a lot of information. Even a small number of responses will likely represent most people's feelings about trust in the organization.

It is, of course, much easier to assess the level of trust in an organization than it is to change the minds of everyone in the organization. Getting people who responded "no" to eventually answer "yes" is probably one of the most difficult tasks for a project manager, especially in a virtual organization. The problem is that once a certain impression is formed, it becomes hard to change, because people do not like change. All companies have in common a remarkable ability to resist change, and changing people's level of trust is no different from trying to convince people to use a new system or process.

> **Best practice:** A trust survey can be done at any time. It should be re-administered periodically to see whether there have been any changes. Consider using a tool like SurveyMonkey to make it easier to collect data and to keep responses anonymous. Tools like this can also be used to track trends in responses over time.

THE PILLARS OF TRUST

Some believe that people are forgetting the basic elements that create success. One such basic element is trust. (Note that success also leads to trust.) In the past, organizations built trust over time without too much difficulty. After all, working day after day with the same people will ultimately lead to most people trusting each other. At the very least, it would lead to people understanding one another.

In a virtual environment, of course, things are different, but many people and organizations act as if communicating by email and phone is the same as or easier than face-to-face contact. In fact, the virtual environment is the hardest environment in which to build trust. Without robust communication and contact, individuals lose touch with one another and often feel isolated and alone.

> **Best practice:** Most people would agree that trust is earned. Reflect on what you can do each day to earn the trust of those involved in the project and in the virtual project organization. Consider what else you can do to grow trust even more.

Although trust is at the core of a successful organization, and a successful project, project managers often disregard the importance of maintaining relationships and working on soft skills. Project managers often gravitate toward using the same individuals and resources for similar tasks, but over time, these relationships can start to fall apart if they are not properly maintained. They can fall out of synch and out of tune. Too often, budgets, deadlines, obstacles, stakeholders, and other situations overtake projects, and the project manager finds him- or herself without the time necessary to devote to the soft-skill parts of a project.

Research has shown that there is no magic way to build trust in a project team; an important element in creating trust is time. Even though there is no surefire way to create trust, a virtual project manager is more likely to succeed if he or she embodies and encourages in others the eight elements, or pillars, of trust shown in Figure 4-2.

| Communication |
| Predictability |
| Honesty |
| Credibility |
| Passion |
| Courage |
| Competency |
| Integrity |

Figure 4-2:   The Pillars of Trust

Pillar One: Communication

The first pillar of trust is communication. Leaders must communicate to create relationships based on trust; leaders who do not remain in contact with their groups have the potential to lose the trust of their teams, and the teams' effectiveness may decline (Cascio 2000; Handy 1995; O'Connor 2000).

Research has shown that the most robust form of communication—and the one that is most likely to build trust—is one-on-one personal interaction in which the parties consider themselves equals, despite their position in the organizational hierarchy. When equals communicate, they can freely exchange ideas, creating opportunities for improvement. Much less is accomplished when a manager simply orders a team member to do something.

> **Best practice:** Make sure that the virtual project management office is willing and able to pay for periodic travel so that the project manager can talk in person with project stakeholders.

Pillar Two: Predictability

The second pillar, predictability, is important because it allows team members to understand the project manager's expectations and the needs of the project. People will follow a predictable project manager—usually because they understand his or her expectations. This is a lesson that project managers must take to heart and apply: the less accessible they are, the less predictable they are, and the less their team members will want to follow them. These team members are not actively trying to usurp their managers—they simply do not know what is expected of them.

We all know that it is easier to find an unfamiliar location when driving in full daylight than it is at night. The darkness can obscure street signs and landmarks. If we apply this metaphor to leadership, we might say that a leader whose expectations are clear is easy to follow. If his expectations are vague and shadowy, people may have a difficult time following him.

> **Best practice:** Think about the people you trust, and consider why you trust them. How can you encourage people in the virtual project organization to display the same trust-building traits?

Pillar Three: Honesty

The third pillar of trust is honesty. Quite simply, project managers must be honest. Honesty is about telling the whole truth. Project managers need to pass along all of the information that is available. Too often, people in organizations tell half-truths and spin stories to make them sound better. In the end, this kind of spin control is obvious to others and is actually worse than lying. Telling half-truths makes a person appear dishonest. Project managers should either learn to tell the whole story or say nothing at all. Telling others that you cannot talk about a situation is better than passing along a partial story.

> **Best practice:** Always tell the truth. Someone is always listening.

A project manager who understands people and their needs will be honest with them. Related to this, the project manager must demonstrate and embody concern for others, both on a professional level and often on a personal level, too. A leader that cares for the whole person is one with whom people will learn to be at ease. People want to be around those who put the needs of the group above the needs of the individual.

Pillar Four: Credibility

The fourth pillar is credibility, the ability of a leader to influence his or her constituency based on the leader's personal values and reputation. A credible leader does what he says he will do and tells others about what he does. Credibility is also about doing the right thing at the right time. It is not to be confused with honesty, for honesty is about telling the truth, while credibility is about taking action based on what one believes. An honest person will tell the truth, but a credible person will act on those personal truths at every opportunity.

> **Best practice:** Working with others builds familiarity, which helps grow trust. Try to get people to collaborate on small projects or initiatives so that they will be familiar with one

> another. This will go a long way to help build their credibility with others in the virtual project organization.

Pillar Five: Passion

The fifth pillar is passion. Making a convincing argument for a cause you believe in is an expression of passion. A leader must display passion for the task and passion for the project. Beyond the project, a successful project manager must also express an interest in the team, the organization, and the community. Expressing these passions will set a high standard that others will want to follow.

> **Best practice:** Passionate people want to work together. Help create cohesion in the organization by giving people chances to collaborate. In a virtual project management organization, everyone eventually will work together on one project or another, either directly or indirectly. Bringing people together now will help you achieve goals faster in the future, as less time will be spent on forming the team; teams will develop organically.

Pillar Six: Courage

The sixth pillar of trust is courage: the willingness to stand up for one's beliefs, challenge others, and admit mistakes. It is very important for project managers to have the courage of their convictions and the courage to stand up for those beliefs, even when doing so is difficult or they go against those of the majority. They do not care if others agree; what they want is for others to at least listen and consider their opinion. Courageous people also have an ability to change, even if they resisted change before.

Pillar Seven: Competency

The seventh pillar of trust is competency. A leader must be competent in her role, and she should have a high degree of expertise in a particular area of the project. She does not need to excel or even be competent in every role on a project, but she must understand the work to be done on a high level. For example, the project manager does not have to be the best coder, but she must at least understand the purpose of the coders' work. Without some level of technical competency, a leader may not be seen as a doer. She might be seen as someone who can issue orders but cannot execute anything on her own. This can breed resentment; others will wonder how the leader attained the position in the first place.

> **Best practice:** Actively seek out professional training to remain competent. Knowing yesterday's technology will not be helpful in tomorrow's business environment. Training should never stop—there is always more to learn.

Pillar Eight: Integrity

The eighth and final pillar of trust is integrity. A project manager with integrity respects himself, the team, and others; more specifically, he respects others' beliefs and the personal culture of individuals and the team. He acts with restraint, and he rises with the tide instead of trying to force back a rising sea of change. Because he makes an effort to do the right thing for the team, he is an accepted part of any decision-making process. Others will trust him and will want to consult him when problems arise and include him when rewards come.

> **Best practice:** Always do the best that you can for the team. Think of the team as often as possible, and make sure management knows that team members also deserve rewards. Those who take care of others will be taken care of later.

Focusing on these pillars is not the only way to build trust, but the pillars are certainly some of the best practices available to a virtual project manager. Too often, other ways of creating trust take more time than the project manager has. Trust must be built quickly to make a project successful. Consistent success is based on the ability to deploy a trusted team that is able to hit the ground running on a new project.

> **Best practice:** Trust is built through every interaction. It's essential to make a point of regularly communicating with project team members, as one cannot build up real trust on a deadline. Connecting with everyone in the virtual project organization will help them feel supported.

ASSESSING TRUST

A trust checklist can help identify the elements of trust that exist and that are lacking in an organization. The checklist in Figure 4-3 offers 40 sample questions that are related to the pillars of trust discussed above. To assess yourself and your organization, choose the most accurate response from these five: 1 – Strongly disagree, 2 – Somewhat disagree, 3 – Neutral, 4 – Somewhat agree, 5 – Strongly agree. (Note, affirmative answers are not necessarily good and negative answers are not necessarily bad.)

Communication

1C)   I find it difficult to mingle in an unknown environment.

2C)   I like to pass along information to others, even when the information is not positive.

3C)   My contact list is one of the first things I would grab during a fire.

4C)   I enjoy meeting new people.

5C)   I find that interacting with others improves my critical thinking.

Predictability

1P)   Others know what I am thinking before I open my mouth.

2P)   People find me to be very consistent.

3P)   I make sure people know the consequences of their actions.

4P)   Others know how I will react to any decision that I am not involved in.

5P)   I make sure that others know what needs to be done so it is done right the first time.

Honesty

1H)   Others find that I am credible.

2H)   People believe what I say when I say it.

3H)   I manage others with integrity.

4H)   I prefer to work in a positive environment.

5H)   I prefer to share my ideas with others than keep them to myself.

Credibility

1D)   Team members believe that I am making the right decisions.

2D)   I believe that being credible is important to the organization.

3D)   Others feel that I do what I say.

4D)   I want others to operate in an ethical manner.

5D)   Others feel that my true character is unquestionably honest.

Passion

1P)   I do not relax until I know the job is complete.

2P)   I have often been accused of beating a dead horse.

3P)   I have never failed in any task.

4P)   If at first you don't succeed, try, try again.

5P)   You only fail if you quit.

Courage

1R)   Gut feelings and intuition are a large part of success.

2R)   I trust the solutions I come up with, and I follow through with them.

3R)   I never seek advice from others.

4R)   I can learn from almost anyone.

5R)   Listening is more important than speaking.

Competency

1M)   I ensure that team members are challenged by current assignments.

2M)   I am able to empower and develop others.

3M)   I share my goals for leading the organization with others.

4M)   The most valuable resource in this organization is its people.

5M)   Others find that I am very skilled in at least one area.

Integrity

1Y)   I get things done at all costs, no matter the method.

2Y)   My number-one job goal is to continually increase my salary and benefits.

3Y)   I adjust what facts I tell my subordinates so they are not demoralized.

4Y)   I must win no matter what obstacles are in the way.

5Y)   Honesty is the best policy, as long as being honest is in the best interest of the organization.

Figure 4-3:   Trust Checklist

MANAGING POLITICS

Technology has created numerous ethical and political issues in business. Technology has facilitated the virtual environment; politics make it more complex. The project manager must accept that politics affect even the virtual environment and learn either to become a political leader in his or her organization or to become a political follower. The project manager who chooses to ignore company politics can find him- or herself a political victim. Projects by their nature are political. Project managers need to use soft skills to convince stakeholders to support a project that may or may not suit their particular needs. In fact, the project may take the organization back a step or cause a downsizing. The project manager needs to deal with the stakeholders and by default becomes involved in politics.

Political Leader

A political leader advertises her projects, which is important in a virtual environment because project teams might not be able to have water cooler chats with others in the organization. When there is no regular social contact between employees, projects that are not promoted can be forgotten. People cannot be part of a great project if no one knows about the project! Leaders who talk up their work will "sell" more—attract more interest—than those who do not seek out "customers."

Political Follower

A political follower makes sure that his or her projects fulfill the objectives of the organization. Projects considered integral to the organization's overall strategy are more likely to gain support and be successful.

Political Victim

Project managers who do not bother to advertise their projects, then learn that the projects are not fully supported by the organization, become political victims. Sometimes a project manager becomes so caught up in saving an over-budget or late project that he forgets that the project is part of the bigger picture: the organization. If a project is not integrated into the organization, the project manager might find himself out of a project—and even out of a job.

TRUST PITFALLS

There are two common pitfalls regarding trust. These often lead to the failure of virtual teams.

- Managers often believe that a successful team should be left alone.
- Sometimes managers think that trust is permanent rather than transient.

Once the manager of a virtual team feels that the team has come together and is functioning effectively, he may believe that there is little else left to do, other than to keep out of the way. Although this hands-off approach could be an effective method for handling a face-to-face team, a virtual team requires additional contact to keep it together and functioning. It is not easy for a manager to continue to monitor and communicate regularly with the team, but this is the only effective way to maintain unity and trust.

Although it is essential for the virtual project manager to monitor the team, he must learn to communicate in a manner that is not intrusive. He must trust that the team will make the right decisions. At the same time, it is important that team members feel able to make the right decisions without always checking in.

Regarding the second pitfall, the truth is that trust needs to be built up on a regular basis. Trust is more like a checking account than like a savings account—the money in the account gets spent and must be replenished. It is not saved for a long period of time. A project manager must learn to continuously fill the account in order to keep trust up in the group.

Best practice: Trust grows in unusual places and at unusual times. Make sure to believe in others during difficult times. Most people want to be very successful, so make sure to give everyone a chance to be very successful. Remember that without visual cues, it will be difficult to communicate effectively, so give your fellow team members the benefit of the doubt, especially during startup.

As more companies build successful virtual organizations, they develop best practices that project managers can harness. Companies that fail to adapt to these organizational changes or cannot leverage the best practices will disappear. Regardless of how the virtual environment evolves, all experts agree that a virtual environment can succeed only when the people within it trust one another. Trust connects people to the project, the organization, and the VPMO. It is what keeps a group together through good times and difficult times and increases a project's chance of success. Virtual organizations that dismiss the importance of trust will most likely fail (Cascio 2000; Hage and Powers 1992;

Kezsbom 2000). Virtual project managers can help build trust by creating a feeling of community on the project team, but the real keys to trust-building are success and time. It is also beneficial for project managers to model and encourage in others eight pillars of trust: communication, predictability, honesty, credibility, passion, courage, competency, and integrity.

Chapter 5

CHANGE

Change is the great equalizer in society, for it creates a new set of rules in life and in organizations. Organizational change can make an experienced person who is valued by an organization into a novice. This can be difficult to accept and is often resisted fiercely by those who are most adversely affected by the change. In the past, workers, soldiers, and seamen were promoted for following orders and moving forward toward their assigned goal. Now, change happens so quickly that rarely will a person be able to follow a straight path towards a goal. Today, it is important to move with change, rather than try to resist it in an attempt to stay on a set path.

A metaphor can help explain the elements of organizational change. Change can be described as a lumberjack with an axe. The lumberjack represents the change agent. The axe represents the stakeholders affected by the change, while the tree represents the old process that will be changed.

- **Lumberjack.** The lumberjack is the agent of change. This agent can be a new person, a new process, or new technology; regardless, the agent of change will cause organizational ripples that will create a new reality. In terms of this metaphor, the change agent—the lumberjack—alters the landscape of the forest. This can be scary to people, as they must watch their old resources be "cut away" in the name of progress.

> **Best practice:** Everyone fears the unknown. Communicate change in advance so that everyone sees it coming. Unless it is a surprise party, few people enjoy surprises.

- **Axe.** The axe is the vehicle for the change—usually, the people that are affected by the change. When a change in, say, technology is made, the reality is that the *people* who will use the technology must change. Technology is just a tool that must be wielded by people, just as the axe must be driven by someone.

- **Tree**. The tree is the old way or process. The tree will not go down easy; the lumberjack will have to chop at it for a while to finally bring it down. Old processes or ways do not go quietly. Individuals will resist and try to keep standing against the change. Though the tree is a formidable obstacle, a lumberjack with an axe is more than a match to bring it down.

RESPONDING TO CHANGE

Change is a difficult process for everyone, but it cannot be avoided. Regardless of our role, career, or organization, everyone will have to handle change several times in their lives. Some changes make us better, such as getting married. Some changes are negative or at least very challenging. A good project manager can try to make any change easier on people by announcing to them when the change is imminent.

Change is particularly hard on people who are not involved in planning the change and do not understand its purpose. Planting crops connects farmers to the harvest. People in organizations are no different: if they are not involved in the plans for a change that will affect them, they are less likely to embrace the change because they feel disconnected, and problems will arise. People may feel helpless, or they may not believe that the change is permanent. The more people are involved in the planning of change, the less likely they are to resist it when it is implemented. Prudent organizations take the time to communicate the benefits of change to individuals to make sure that they are part of the process.

There are three other common reasons people resist change:

- **The change is not explained.** People will resist more if they are not informed of changes ahead of time. People do not like to be forced to do the unknown and may try to circumvent the change.
- **The purpose of the change is not understood.** If people don't understand the long-term vision behind the change,

they may assume that it is just an experiment. This is particularly likely in organizations where changes tend to be made according to political whims. The change will not seem credible, and people may assume that the good ol' days will be back again soon, so there is no reason to go along with the change.

- **Disruption of workflow.** Finally, the disruption to workflow makes all change unsettling. When people have become used to performing functions in a certain manner, then things change, it is very difficult to make this leap without support. The organization must offer training and make other efforts to minimize the disruption.

> **Best practice:** Learning and change are connected. One must connect change to learning to reduce resistance because training is conceptually linked to improvement. Training should be treated as a benefit, not a punishment, to improve the likelihood that people will accept the change.

People tend to react to change in one of three general ways: as change makers, change breakers, or change takers. Keep these three archetypes in mind when you are planning a change so that you can respond appropriately. Having a prepared plan will help you address people's individual concerns and comments.

Change Maker

This person is usually a leader in the organization. He is a driven individual who wants to change some aspect of the organization—but he may not have changes *other* people want to make on his agenda, especially if those changes will affect him. He wants to reach his objective at the expense of other people's objectives. (Remember this point: today's change maker can become tomorrow's change breaker or change taker.)

The only way to deal with the change maker is through negotiation. Avoidance will not work for long; the change maker will eventually pin down everyone whom the change will affect. Because he is single-minded about the change, you may be able to benefit in some way from being agreeable to the change. Make the most of the negotiation, because the change maker will hold to his end of the bargain as long as you do.

Change Breaker

Change breakers resist change. Be prepared to encounter a lot of different kinds of change breakers. They may resist change directly or indirectly, overtly or covertly, even when they know there is no choice in the matter. You must come up with a firm plan to deal with these naysayers.

There are several approaches to working with the change breaker. Three methods are applicable in the virtual environment: force, negotiation, and inclusion.

- **Force.** Forcing the change breaker to accept the change sounds like the most satisfying way of dealing with him, but it is generally regarded as the least effective. One can force anyone to do anything, but that does not mean that he will do it with any degree of fervor. The moment that he is not monitored, you can be sure that he will go back to doing things as they were done before the change. No one wants to be forced to do anything, so this course should be taken in the fewest cases or as a last resort.

- **Negotiation.** Negotiating with the change breaker is often the best course. It will allow her to feel as if she is part of the process. She will benefit in some way for going along with the change, and it is likely that she will continue to embrace the change if the incentive is good enough. Consider offering positive incentives, such as rewards and salary increases, rather than threatening negative incentives such as job loss or demotion. Be sure to have a solid negotiation plan before confronting the change breaker. A protracted negotiation creates problems; the change breaker will complain to others about the change until the negotiation is final. Make sure to complete the negotiation quickly and effectively.

- **Inclusion.** Inclusion is best when it is done early in the change process. When you include potential change breakers in change planning, you can offer them a way to become a change taker. Inclusion can also be a successful strategy when it is used later in the change process. Involving a change breaker in a part of the process that interests her or in an area that will benefit her can help convert her into a change taker.

Consider what the change will do to the individual's job and career. What specific effects will it have? Think about what it would be like to be in her shoes during this change. Once you have identified the effects of the change, then you can determine how to include the change breaker in the change.

Change Taker

A change taker has considered the negatives and positives of the change and has concluded that the change is good and will benefit him. Once a change taker is convinced that the change is positive, he will accept it and move on. Most people resist change initially because they fear or dislike the unknown, so it's unusual for someone to be a change taker from the outset. People are more likely to act as change takers once they understand how a change will benefit them.

> **Best practice:** If you encounter strong resistance to change, openly challenge the other party to change for the good of the company. Sometimes appealing to a person's emotional side helps him to move forward and to stop the negative behavior.

COPING WITH CHANGE

In today's dynamic business world, project managers must be very flexible to meet their clients' needs. Clients are demanding greater results from smaller teams in a shorter amount of time. Projects are becoming increasingly complicated, and specific management tasks are less defined. Project managers are more frequently being tasked with implementing change at all levels of the organization. Because all business assignments are also leadership assignments and can be made into projects, all project managers must learn to master project change leadership.

In general terms, a project is defined by the following elements: the project manager, the time allotted for the project, the project management system, and a completion date (Krajewski and Ritzman, 1996). Although all of these elements are important, the critical factor is always the ability of the project manager to cope with change. A great virtual project manager can always deliver exceptional results, no matter how difficult the project is. To understand how these successful virtual project managers achieve great results, we must review the strategies they use to cope with change. Figure 5-1 outlines four strategies for coping with change: responsibility, planning, speed, and contingency.

Best practice: The engineering symbol for change is Δ. Use this symbol to mark anything that should change to better support the virtual project management office. When you see the symbol in your notes, you will be reminded of the need for change.

Responsibility

The first strategy is responsibility. According to Admiral Hyman J. Rickover, "A project manager can delegate authority but not

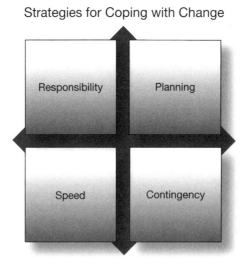

Figure 5-1: Strategies for Coping with Change

responsibility. Responsibility is indivisible. When something goes wrong and you cannot find the specific individual to put your finger on, then you have never really had the responsibility" (Eigen and Siegel 1989, p. 227). This quote applies not just to project management but to change. Understanding who is responsible is necessary if change is to actually happen. If no one is responsible for the change, nothing gets done because there is no incentive to achieve the desired results.

Note that the person responsible should also be the person with full authority to execute the change. Less-seasoned individuals may accept responsibility without having full authority, but they are likely to fail in carrying out the change. Anyone without authority is at a serious disadvantage when trying to implement a change, and this type of situation should be avoided at all costs.

> **Best practice:** Always lead from the front. One must always change first in order to expect others to change. Leading by example is very important in a virtual project management office because your actions will be observed by so many different stakeholders.

Planning

The second strategy for coping with change is planning the path. No one would ever jump into a car and start driving to a new destination without consulting others for directions or reviewing a map, but many project managers address change in just this manner. Successful projects never "just happen" to complete on time and on budget. They follow a preestablished path that eventually ends in the desired result.

Whenever a change is expected, a good project manager should spend considerable time planning every dimension of the projected change in advance. One must understand what the end result of the change will be to create a plan that will support that end. Planning means giving thought to the path and the destination. Structured planning serves to organize thoughts and tasks while also illustrating the change and directing people toward it. The project manager should also create a timeline to monitor progress toward the change. Monitoring progress is the only way to keep from falling behind schedule.

> **Best practice:** A plan should never become static; it should always be in motion. You should constantly monitor progress in order to determine where you are along the path. Start with a plan, but modify the plan to take advantage of whatever new resources are found along the way. The road to success is not a single path—there may be a multitude of different options.

Speed

The third strategy for coping with change is speed. Sometimes change needs to be completed swiftly in order to meet project deadlines. Complete changes in the shortest amount of time possible. Change that drags out for a long time will become like a dead albatross around the neck of an organization. People who are paralyzed by analysis or who cannot navigate the quagmire of organizational politics are doomed to experience the "unbearable longness" of change. Changes fail because projects are frozen by politics or committees more often than for any other reason. Learn to leverage all resources to support a speedy change.

> **Best practice:** Moving faster is almost always better. If you wait too long to make a decision, then the opportunity has probably already passed by. Make sure to always move faster than the client. If the client has to push the project, then the VPMO is not doing its job.

Contingency

Contingency is the fourth and final coping-with-change strategy. "Plan and prepare for the unexpected" is the mantra of the successful project manager. What might happen if the change fails, the change is delayed, the change is resisted? No change will progress exactly according to the original schedule, so be ready to adapt to unforeseen circumstances. Always consider the worst-case scenario and develop a plan to cope with those situations. Keep in mind that anyone can steer a ship when the seas are calm, but it takes an exceptional master to keep a ship afloat when there are 40-foot waves and freezing spray.

There are always alternatives to solving any problem; it is just a matter of identifying them before making the change. Remember, just because a solution addresses the problem, that does not mean that it is the only solution. List a number of alternative approaches, and keep this list available during the project. It is much easier to pre-plan than it is to try to solve problems under time pressure.

We can see that all of the four strategies for managing change are important for success. Our advice can be summed up in a few points:

- Focus and planning are two of the keys to successful change. Continually focus on the goal and travel as close to the planned path as possible.
- When a leader loses his resolve, one can be sure that others will abandon the change.
- Always remember that the goal is to complete the project to the highest possible standard, regardless of how many times the project goal may have changed. You may have to reject changes to ensure the project maintains its quality.

Just following these strategies will not guarantee successful change, but ignoring them will certainly contribute to the failure of any change.

> **Best practice:** Dreams about work often are reflections of one's insecurities or anxieties. The next time you have a dream about work, think about what caused the dream. What can you change to eliminate the source of the insecurities or anxieties? Keep in mind that if the situation you are anxious about is affecting other people, someone else may make a change if you don't—and that change might not be so favorable to you.

SUPPORTING CHANGE

Organizationally speaking, there are two systems to support change. First, change can be reinforced by relationships between individuals—that is, customers and sponsors (see Figure 5-2). The second

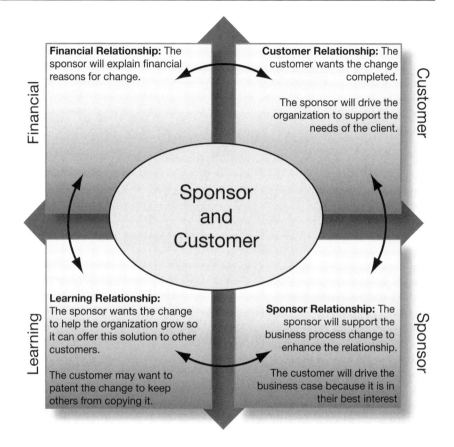

Figure 5-2:   Change and Organizational Relationships

system is more metaphorical: a story or history surrounding the change is created to make it part of the organizational culture.

The Sponsor-Customer Relationship and the Sponsor's Role

Many organizations subscribe to the belief that all changes must have an owner—a sponsor—to be successful. The sponsor owns the change and all the responsibilities associated with it. There is significant merit to this belief, but there is more to the story. Change does need an owner if it is to succeed, but the customer— the internal or external person who benefits from the change—is equally important. This organizational relationship is what makes the change succeed; it will be reviewed later in greater detail.

For any change project, a clear sponsor must be defined. Occasionally the sponsor and the customer are the same person, but the virtual project management office does not have to get involved if this is the case. If, for example, a department or team lead is making an internal team change to improve her group, this is best handled internally, according to the leader's own leadership style. Here, we focus on situations in which the sponsor and the customer are different people.

The sponsor must understand the customer's needs for any change to succeed. Change without this kind of understanding is simply change without a purpose. New project managers sometimes attempt to leave their mark on an organization by rearranging things that were already working. If there is no clear reason for making a change, people may assume that the project manager is simply trying to push her own agenda. Assuming that this is not the case, project managers must make sure that everyone in the virtual organization understands the needs of the customer so that others can see that the change has a purpose and meaning.

> **Best practice:** The customer's needs are paramount. Know the customer and make sure your change project addresses those needs.

The sponsor of the change must also have sufficient authority to complete the project. Authority is particularly important in a virtual organization because people will not see you struggling if you need help. A sponsor who lacks authority cannot be successful, and the customer will suffer accordingly.

It is also critical that the sponsor carefully manage the scope of the project. Too often, when a virtual project begins, the project manager has sufficient authority to complete the tasks at hand, but when the scope starts to creep up, he find himself trapped—suddenly, other layers of approval are required. This will slow the project down and can put it in jeopardy. The project has grown, but the deadline has not changed—and now additional approvals or the involvement of other parties is necessary for completion. This situation, which we call the VPMO approval delay time trap, is mapped out in Figure 5-3.

When a project is growing, the worst possible thing to do would be to slow down the process, yet this is what many organizations

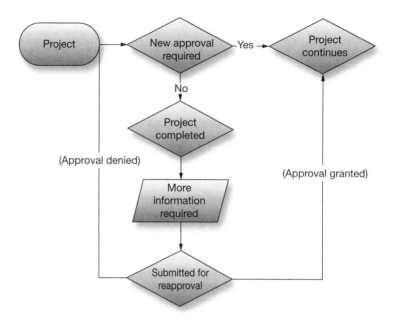

Figure 5-3: VPMO Approval Delay Time Trap

do. Consider that as the scope of the project increases, costs will increase; at the same time, the project's visibility and importance in the organization will also rise. As spending increases to support the project, more eyes will be on it, and more people will want to be part of the process. The project manager was originally given significant fiscal responsibility, but now that the project has grown, he may no longer have the requisite level of authority to keep the project going. This will cause a cascade effect that will slow down the project at a time it needs to be as nimble as possible. This scenario plays out too often and in too many organizations, so it is best to consider the possibility of scope creep at the start of the project to avoid this time trap.

Metaphors

Information is now the currency of virtual organizations, and the organizations that can align that currency with their own values will be the ones that can achieve continued success. Virtual organizations offer new challenges to leadership and teams; as they confront the limitations of the virtual world, they have opportunities to become more than their traditional brick-and-mortar counterparts. Metaphors—compelling stories that others can connect to—can help them do this. Metaphors "give us the opportunity to stretch our thinking and deepen our understanding, thereby allowing us to see things in new ways and to act in new ways" (Morgan 1998, p. 5).

Metaphors are intended to inspire people to make decisions based on the organization's core values. They can be a powerful means of virtual management. There is no limit to the number of metaphors or stories that an organization might use, but it's important to make sure that the positive stories continue, while the negative stories disappear over time.

A strong story that is rooted in organizational values could be used to help resolve problems without the direct intervention of the virtual project manager. If the project manager is brought in to correct the problem, the virtual team will learn to wait for help rather than take corrective action. Virtual teams will become more adept at resolving conflict if they are allowed to do so on their own.

An example from history can help prove this point. Before the establishment of the United States, England controlled its colonies by appointing autonomous governors, who were to perform certain duties as required by the crown. The governors were charged with handling the day-to-day business of maintaining the peace and keeping the colonies relatively secure. These governors had great latitude in how they implemented their rule, as long as the laws of the crown were followed and taxes were collected and sent back.

A project manager who oversees a large multinational project is similar to a colonial governor, and the way the governors managed their responsibilities is a good example for virtual project managers to follow. The virtual project manager cannot be the one to handle every disruption. She cannot automatically insert herself to resolve problems, as she could on a local project. Just as a colonial governor would have been asked to preside over a legal case involving individuals that had a dispute, the project manager will step in at the team's request only when it is really necessary.

In lieu of the project manager's constant presence, when conflicts or unexpected situations arise in the virtual environment, organizational metaphors can offer guidance. The legendary Nordstrom employee "handbook"—a single card—offered simple guidance to cover all circumstances (Spector and McCarthy 2005; see Figure 5-4). Similarly, a metaphor is a general allegory that provides guidance in various situations.

Welcome to Nordstrom*

We're glad to have you with our Company. Our number one goal is to provide outstanding customer service. Set both your personal and professional goals high. We have great confidence in your ability to achieve them.

Nordstrom Rules

Rule #1: Use your best judgment in all situations. There will be no additional rules.

Please feel free to ask your department manager, store manager, or division general manager any question at any time.

---

*Reprinted with permission from John Wiley & Sons, Inc.

Figure 5-4:   The Nordstrom Employee "Handbook"

Consider how a metaphor can shape an organization. For years, a story has circulated about the customer who successfully returned a set of tires to a Nordstrom store for a refund—even though the retail chain has never sold tires. Though the veracity of the story has never been confirmed (no one from Nordstrom has come forward with the actual tires and the refund receipt), it is now a piece of customer-service legend. Nordstrom has long been known for top-flight customer service, and this story serves to offer a clear guideline for everyone in the organization: "The customer is always right, even when they are wrong."

This story has been told and retold at various times and by various people, yet the core of the story remains the same. The details may change with the telling, but the legend continues to grow. In the end, it does not matter if the story is apocryphal or not. What matters is that it has aligned the organization towards a certain goal, and it offers Nordstrom customers a reason to choose that company over others. Consider the benefit of this story to the company. Perhaps Nordstrom did refund the cost of a set of tires to a particularly persistent or confused person and had to absorb the loss—yet the marketing value of the story is enormous.

Keep this in mind when considering what stories are worthy of being retold. The power of storytelling or metaphor-making is clear: it can help focus an organization toward a particular goal or direction without any kind of management direction or intervention. A story like this will certainly pay dividends to employees; it tells them exactly what must be done. They do not have to wait until a manager is available to ask for permission to take action.

BRANDING CHANGE

To encourage a virtual project management organization to embrace virtual elements to a greater degree, it is necessary to adopt a successful change management strategy. Creating a project brand is one element of such a strategy. The development of a virtual project management office should be branded to give the project and the change an identity. Furthermore, there should be a timeline associated with the brand. Having a deadline will help move the project toward its goals, and it will better focus the brand.

Branding any change, including a change toward a virtual project organization, is a three-step process:

1. Name the change.

2. Create an identity for the brand (identify its goals).

3. Integrate the brand into the organizational culture.

Creating a Name

The first step in branding a change is to create a name for the change within the organization. When considering a name for a project, there is a temptation to call the project something generic, such as "virtual change" or "virtual project." Instead, consider a more creative name that will be more memorable. In acronym-heavy organizations, perhaps an acronym, such as VCP for "virtual change program," would be appropriate. To connect the deadline with the project, you can add a number at the end of the acronym to reflect the due date of the project—for example, you might use the name VCP7 for a project that is due in July.

Some organizations tend to use symbolic names. A virtual change project could be called "Golden Gate" to pull the symbolism of change as a bridge to a new place. Here, too, a number can be added at the end of the name to indicate the due date of the project. This project could be branded "Golden Gate12" if it is due at the end of the year. Historical references or names of animals, rivers, or objects related to the brand impression also work well. For example, a change project could be named "Route 66," "Eagle," "Enterprise," "Wheel," or "(Johnny) Appleseed." Again, a numeric identifier can be added to the name to denote its due date: "Eagle1."

Creating an Identity

The second step is to create an identity for the brand by clearly identifying the goals of the project. Sometimes this just requires making a short list of the high-level deliverables and objectives of the project. These goals can be documented on cards and distributed to all project stakeholders to help remind them of the project's values and goals. Figure 5-5 shows a sample project goal card. Keeping the identity and brand of the project visible is a good way to make sure that people remain focused on the project.

Sometimes a project needs new goals and an identity change because it is struggling in some way. For example, in one organization, a particularly high-profile project was behind schedule. In that organization, projects were numbered, and so the rallying cry became "5989 on time!" In that case, the project's only identity was that it was running late. It needed a new identity that would help speed it up.

Integrating the Project into the Culture

Third, the name and identity of the project must be integrated into the culture of the organization. This is achieved by using the name or acronym of the project in all correspondence about it, both internal and external. The more the name is used, the more that it will be remembered, which in turn will lead to the brand's being integrated into the organizational culture. Consider how powerful brand names like Kleenex, Coke, or Xerox are. These words are often used interchangeably with the generic terms "facial tissue,"

YOUR LOGO
Project Logo

PROJECT NAME

Goal or Value #1

Goal or Value #2

Goal or Value #3

Goal or Value #4

Figure 5-5:   Project Goal Card

"soda" or "photocopy," to the point that people may not even realize that they are brand names.

A brand name and identify are powerful tools, and the virtual organization must take advantage of them. A virtual project management organization lives by successful projects. Great projects become the stuff of legends, and a good legend always has a good name.

Many people remember the Alamo, the site of a battle fought for the independence of Texas. It was important battle fought against impossible odds, yet the defenders never considered surrender. According to the Alamo's visitor center, more than 2.5 million people annually visit the historic location—170 years after the battle was lost. Consider the power of that brand: a lost battle (failed project), yet remembered and visited by millions almost two hundred years after the fact.

Figure 5-6 illustrates the effects of a change on an organization's culture and people. When a stakeholder is able to explain how the elements of change shown in the diagram have affected her and the organization, then the brand has been integrated into the culture.

> **Best practice:** Consider branding even small change initiatives in a VPMO. A name gives life to a project. Remember the Alamo!

We see that branding change is critical to virtual project management success. People identify with brands on a daily basis. If one can make a virtual project into a successful brand, then the concept will be integrated into the organizational culture. Just as people remember the Alamo, they will remember other projects (even the unsuccessful ones) as instructional landmarks for the organization.

DELEGATING CHANGE

People will present requests for change to the manager of a virtual organization every day, but not all changes are necessary. It's

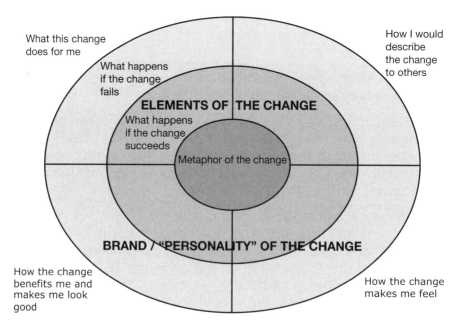

Figure 5-6:   Elements of Change and Its Effects on Culture and People

important to gauge the need for a change before actually taking action. It's also essential to determine who should handle changes. Figure 5-7 shows that the virtual manager should handle only the most important and urgent changes. This will help keep the manager focused on the larger picture of the project.

In most cases, the change should be delegated down to a person who is authorized and most involved. Make sure that the proper person has the authority and ability to make the change. The fewer matters pertaining to change that the virtual manager is directly involved with, the more likely that the project will move forward swiftly. Managers oversee the group and process; they need not always be the person spearheading every element of the project. Keep in mind that delegation does not absolve the virtual manager of responsibility or blame, but it does allow the manager to share the work with others for greater results.

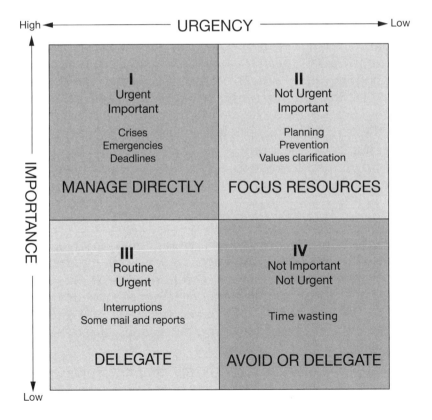

Figure 5-7: Evaluating the Need for and Urgency of Change

Virtual managers should be less involved with the actual changes and more involved in the decision to proceed with change. Although they might be tempted to be involved with every step and process of the project, there is not enough time to do so. For a virtual project to remain efficient, waiting time must be minimized so that the project can keep moving forward. Keep in mind that time is often more important than anything else on a project with a deadline. A deadline can be kept only if the project is continually moving forward. Resources need to be aligned and focused, and stakeholders need to be kept informed. As much as one would like to believe that company politics do not affect a project, in reality they must be observed and addressed. In short, the virtual project must keep moving to achieve success, but this cannot happen if the manager is involved in every aspect.

Everyone Is a Leader

There is a common myth in business that the only person who can truly make a change is the head of the organization, usually the president or CEO of the company. (This is also a common perception in politics; many people believe that change can come only with the election of a new president—as if the president is the only person who can make a change in government.) The reason that this myth is so compelling is that it satisfies people's intrinsic desire to blame someone else for their dissatisfaction. In an organization, it is easy to pin problems on someone who is making big bucks and seems to hold all of the power.

In the virtual project management organization, changes can be happening in multiple locations simultaneously. Working to embrace this kind of complex change is a function of leadership. In a virtual organization, the person responsible for change and for problems is the leader—and the leader is *everyone*. Not the boss, not the human resources manager, not the people who were promoted, but everyone. Of course, this does not mean that everyone is the leader at all times, but it does mean that if one wants change, then one must lead it.

Because it is not possible for people to continually seek direction in a virtual environment, as they might be able to do in a traditional office, people on virtual teams must learn to take the initiative to make the changes necessary in their own areas. But this is difficult—what can ordinary people do to move an organization in a new direction? A four-step process can help: first, learn to recognize the needs associated with the change; make a map or plan for the change; follow up with everyone involved regarding the change; and finally, celebrate the success of the change.

Recognizing Needs

In most cases, change will be an inherent part of a project. For example, implementing a new system will create changes in processes, procedures, and perception. The easiest part of a change like this is typically the technology. The hardest part of change is always the people. New hardware will be configured once and software installed, but people will require multiple training and support sessions in order to make the project a success. What, specifically, will have to be done to make these changes happen?

Planning for Change

Once you know what must be done to successfully implement the change, you must develop a map or plan for change, which will indicate where the organization is and where it should be in the future. A plan may not always result in success, but it will offer an idea of what to expect in the future. The map or plan can take the form of a diagram or chart.

Consider the amount of design and planning that goes into the construction of a new building. Think about the engineering and architectural plans that are developed before any construction is started. Contractors, consultants, and governmental organization will all review these documents before construction is allowed to begin. The same type of care should be taken regarding any organizational change. Most organizational change in a virtual project management organization will require extra planning and care because with less physical contact and proximity, the people involved are more likely to feel distant from the change and may not understand what is expected or embrace the change. Without continual feedback and directional support, it will be difficult for the organization to change. Change is not an easy process, even when it is planned and mapped out, so the more that can be done to explain the process to people, the more likely it is that the change will ultimately be successful.

> **Best practice:** Consider posting the plan for change in a place that all stakeholders can see. This could be in a public area, on the company website, or on a company's intranet.

Following Up

The third step in the process is following up with all the stakeholders affected by the change. You must make contact with them at the beginning of the change, as well as during the change itself, to get their feedback. Communication with stakeholders is essential. It is particularly important to make extra efforts to connect with stakeholders in a virtual environment because options for communication are limited, which makes it harder to connect with all of the relevant people. The more you follow up and the more feedback you gather, the better the change process will go, though you might not be able to integrate feedback and fix the problems people mention right away.

> **Best practice:** Mark follow-ups as a recurring meeting on your planner to make sure that communication with stakeholders happens regularly throughout the process.

It is very difficult to accept harsh or negative feedback during a change process, but one must be willing to listen. Allowing people to vent from time to time can be healthy, and they might have good ideas about how to retain some of the old ways in the midst of change. The implementation of a new software system might provide better tracking and understanding and reporting of key processes and economic indicators, making the organization more competitive. This may be important to senior management, but the data entry clerk, for example, will want to know why there is a new entry process when the old system met her needs. The data entry clerk may not be aware of the system's dependencies and connections. Change often occurs because things need to be done differently in order to support another change down the line.

In a virtual project management organization, everyone can be an architect of change within the organization. Learn how to lead and to change the organization by figuring out what single item could be changed to make a difference.

Celebrating Success

The final step in the process is to celebrate success. Celebrations are important in a virtual project management office because they offer closure, recognize the team for its work, and instill a sense of pride, an important motivator, in the process. Celebrations help team members feel a connection to the project; in turn, they will want to continue working hard in hopes of achieving even greater success.

Change is the hardest concept for people to embrace. Even people who are often open to change will occasionally resist it; everyone will function as a change maker, change breaker, or change taker at some point in their lives. There is no magic method VPMOs can use to help people cope with organizational change, though there are four general strategies for coping with change: responsibility, planning, speed, and contingency. Sponsor-customer relationships, metaphors, and branding the change can reinforce a change as it is implemented and afterwards.

Chapter 6

CULTURE

Culture has been described in many ways, and Schein's definition is still one of the most accurate: Culture is "[a] pattern of shared basic assumptions that [a] group learned as it solved its problems of external adaptation and internal integration that has worked well enough to be considered valid and, therefore, to be taught to new members as the correct way to perceive, think, and feel in relation to those problems" (1992, p. 12). Schein has more recently described culture as a web that binds individuals together such that they have a shared ethos (2004).

UNDERSTANDING CULTURE

We already know that all cultures are different. Even related companies or organizations will have different cultures. Consider that each of us went to different schools growing up. Even if the schools you attended were in the same town or even in the same neighborhood and were similar in certain ways, each school managed to have a unique culture that affected your experience there. As a student, there was little you could do to change the school culture. Now think about the jobs you've held, and consider the culture in each of those firms. Consider how different your experience at a certain company would have been if the culture of that organization had been different.

> **Best practice:** Do not settle for being a spectator. Be integral to the virtual project management office, and be a part of the history of the organization. What would it take to get your company to "retire your number" when you leave?

Organizationally speaking, culture is a force that binds all of us together in a way that is greater than each single person. We might think of it as, in the words of Obi-Wan Kenobi, "an energy field created by all living things. It surrounds us, penetrates us, and binds the galaxy together." Similarly, one can think of culture as the force behind the invisible hand that moves business (Smith 1904). If culture is the force that moves groups of people, one must be able to understand how this force works to create a successful virtual project management office. One must learn how to make the culture support the project management office, rather than allowing the culture to function as an impediment to success.

To understand organizational culture, one needs to understand the elements of culture. Although no two organizational cultures are alike, most successful organizations have at least seven different cultural attributes that contribute to their success: innovation and risk taking, attention to detail, outcome orientation, people orientation, team orientation, aggressiveness, and stability. All firms either promote or discourage these elements; the manner in which an organization handles these attributes defines its culture. We will examine each of these elements to determine how they can affect a culture in order to facilitate cultural change. In essence, a single individual who understand the roots of culture can learn to change it.

ATTRIBUTES OF CULTURE

The following attributes will explain some of the key elements that make up culture:

- Innovation and risk taking
- Attention to detail
- Outcome orientation
- People orientation
- Team orientation
- Aggressiveness
- Stability.

Keep these seven attributes in mind when considering how an organization's culture can impact a VPMO. In a virtual environment, culture determines how individuals act and react when others are not around to monitor them.

Innovation and Risk Taking

An important aspect of organizational culture is the degree of innovation and risk taking that individuals are granted. Organizations that allow individuals to take risks and innovate at any opportunity are those organizations that do not punish people for making mistakes. At the other end of the spectrum, many organizations discourage people from admitting to mistakes and punish those that underachieve, regardless of the circumstances. Where is your organization on this risk-taking scale?

Innovation and risk taking are definitely important in a successful virtual project management office. A lack of innovation and risk taking means that the culture supports complacency. Organizations in which people have an "I'm right, you're wrong" mentality discourage innovation and are not going to remain successful. If a culture is based on the ideas of a select few rather than the ideas of the group, the organization will eventually stagnate. On the other hand, a culture that actively supports innovation and risk taking is one that encourages finding solutions to problems, even when the problems are not impeding the current project.

If you are not sure if your culture supports innovation and risk taking, talk to the successful people in the organization and find out if they have created new processes based on different people's ideas, or if their success comes from devising workarounds to navigate the existing system. Too often individuals learn how to be successful by playing according to the rules of the culture or by doing what is politically expedient, rather than actually finding solutions to the problems. Those who fail to understand the difference between game-playing and real innovation will have difficulty moving the culture forward. Whenever politics trumps progress, one needs to examine the roots of the culture to find out what is holding the organization back.

> **Best practice:** Ask the people in the immediate project group to identify any workarounds that have been developed over time. Review these workarounds and develop a plan to either implement permanent fixes or make the workarounds the new policy.

Attention to Detail

In project management, the devil is in the details. Project success is never achieved by taking a 10,000-foot view of the work. To examine this element of culture, one needs to look at how people in the organization react to small problems. Are they escalated to ensure that quality is maintained? In organizations that focus on attention to detail, top quality is always important and even minor details are handled as a project crisis. Some organizations would consider this a waste of time and effort, but attention to detail is a matter of quality. If quality is compromised, shouldn't someone say something about it? Is the goal of the project to deliver the minimum according to the specifications, or is the goal of the project to deliver a client-centric and impressive product?

It is true that there is always a cost associated with producing the best possible project, but a focus on quality increases the likelihood of producing a great project. When was the last time that a client was impressed with a project that achieved the minimum possible standards?

> **Best practice:** Consider what more your team can do to "wow" a client. Make little changes that might make a big difference in the final deliverables.

Outcome Orientation

Project-based companies are driven by outcome. The ultimate goal is the successful launch of a project. All areas are measured by outcome, and the results you produce are the single most important factor in the direction of your career at a project-based company. The company demands results and, more importantly, it demands results beyond established expectations. Careers are made or broken by results. Those who perform under difficult circumstances are rewarded; those who do not perform are deployed in another location.

> **Best practice:** Find a way to reward people who are successful despite difficult circumstances. People who are willing to work to achieve goals during difficult times are worth having around for future projects.

People Orientation

Organizations are made up of people, obviously, and people are what make projects successful. Successful projects are launched by outstanding people. A project manager must remember that the people make the culture; the culture does not make the people. Too often, people in organizations feel that the culture of the organization is letting them down. If the culture is failing, then the people are failing. And when the people are failing, everyone in the organization must look to see what can be done better.

> **Best practice:** Who are the best people in your VPMO? Know their strengths and weaknesses so that you can make the most of their strengths.

Team Orientation

Teams are very important in a virtual organization's culture. The more that people feel that they are part of a team, the better off the organization will be because the feeling of being included will generate loyalty and trust. However, certain team behaviors can be destructive. Sometimes people affiliate with smaller teams more readily than larger ones or the organization as a whole. When smaller teams become more important than the larger team, particularly destructive turf wars can erupt. Turf-sensitive groups are less interested in building consensus with other groups than they are in marking their territory.

For example, if resources are limited, smaller groups might take exception to sharing with others. This can create an atmosphere of animosity and create incentives for groups to actively undermine one another. This negative behavior can destroy an organization as groups look out for themselves, rather than for the whatever's best for the entire company.

> **Best practice:** Consider naming the team to create a stronger identity. Sometimes a corny name will help people better identify with the group. Never underestimate the power of calling a group something goofy like "Chaotic People's Republic."

Aggressiveness

Although many people have a negative perception of aggressiveness and favor collaborative, group-oriented approaches, in any organization there is a need for people who are willing to lead. One cannot ignore the effectiveness of aggressiveness in an organization's culture. Without aggressiveness, there is no risk taking and no innovation.

There are countless studies that show that our heroes are sports figures, astronauts, adventurers, explorers, celebrities, even some politicians—individuals who have achieved greatness in some way. (In some cases, our heroes were not even entirely successful in their endeavors, but they gave their best effort.) I have never heard of a study that found a single individual who considered Congress, the United Nations, or the International Olympic Committee to be heroes. People accept that teams and diversity are powerful organizational forces in society, yet few organizations are heroes worthy of our attention. Why is this? The reason is not so clear. People understand the purpose and benefits of teams, and some may be very involved in sports teams, leagues, or institutions, yet we seem to understand that it is the force of one that can make a difference.

Aggressiveness is related to the concept of a single individual making a difference. If one person can take an aggressive position to move a project forward, then a single person can make a difference. Oftentimes this means asserting a new direction or course for the project. Aggressiveness is like the rudder on a ship; the rudder is in the back of the vessel but it makes the front of the vessel turn. Hence, aggressiveness operates like a rudder. For example, the greater the angle of the rudder in the back, the greater the angle of the turn of the ship in the front. Although many people feel that one person cannot move a culture, the reality is that each of us can change the culture more than we want to believe. Sometimes, all that is needed to change the culture is a change in a single person's behavior. The moment that one person changes, she becomes a model for others' behavior. When others see the change, they can ignore the change, observe it, or adopt it.

Stability

Even in times of change, people want to believe that their organization is stable and will still be there in the future. This is particularly important in a project-based organization because individuals are constantly moving from project to project, and there can be a lot of unrest between projects. If the organization is growing, then there will always be a new project to move to, but if the organization is shrinking or new projects are scarce, then people will worry about stability.

> **Best practice:** What steps have been taken to make your virtual project management office stable? Make a list of what can be done to help give people the feeling of stability, and see how many of these action items can be completed in the next month. Positive change starts now, and making people feel secure is often more important than giving them a raise.

COPING WITH DYSFUNCTIONAL CULTURE

In many organizations, project managers can only do so much to impact the overarching culture of the organization. At the same time, an organization's global culture will affect its projects, but it does not need to dominate the projects. If the culture is positive, it might be easiest to allow the culture to define the project. However, this kind of approach has some inherent weaknesses. If the project manager does not direct the culture, then the culture might resist the project. For example, not all team members might want the project to succeed. If the culture is not a positive one, the project manager will usually simply need to cope with the culture in order to survive the project. It is this kind of situation that we will discuss here, because all project managers, regardless of how skilled they are, will one day find themselves in a situation in which the overall culture is not helping the project, and they will need to develop some kind of coping strategy. This does not mean that coping is the only way out, but it is one way to get better results from the people on the project.

A project manager must accept that sooner or later, at least part of any virtual team will be mildly to severely dysfunctional. Dysfunctional organizations are less productive, less efficient, and less organized, and they have more problems. Many times, when organizations notice a drop in productivity, they add new people to the troubled team. However, a severely dysfunctional organization will continue to experience a noticeable drop in total productivity, despite an increase in staff. In the most severely dysfunctional organizations, employees, as a whole, feel "beat up" by the circumstances that have prevailed over a long period of time. These organizations may have some or all of the following problems:

- There is no history or culture within the organization because of multiple reorganizations.
- Employees feel powerless and despairing because they do not know if they will have a job tomorrow or who their boss will be.
- Employees believe that management cares preeminently about the customer, to the detriment of the company and the employees. They think, "The company doesn't care if my skills are up-to-date. I am a billable asset, and therefore a revenue stream. They do not care about me." Employees who feel this way tend to disconnect from the company.

A common thread across dysfunctional organizations is a lack of contemporary rituals. Without rituals, there is no commonality or sense of community to bind employees together.

CHANGING CULTURE

Many people believe that there is little that can be done to move culture. What is closer to the truth is that it is extremely hard to change culture. Because it is very hard to change culture, many people stop there and conclude that it is not possible to do so. But organizational culture is constantly changing.

When people think about their organization's culture, they often focus on the larger elements of culture that have always been there, without considering the smaller pieces that contribute to the whole. This tendency helps reinforce the idea that culture cannot change. But there is one important system that can help reinforce a cult ure: peer pressure. The term *peer pressure* has a negative connotation because it is often connected with negative behaviors such as smoking or drug use. Yet peer pressure is an irresistible force in organizations and can manipulate people into doing previously unthinkable acts.

> **Best practice:** Peer pressure can be used to help people to fall into line with a project. Consider telling stakeholders about how others have supported the project. For example, one project stakeholder delivered pizza to people working on the project. Another stakeholder heard about this and did the same thing the next week. Just hearing about an act of kindness can encourage people to perform a further act of kindness in a pay-it-forward kind of way.

It is speculated that the indigenous people of Mesoamerica were the first to use spicy peppers for medicinal purposes, but more importantly, as flavoring for food. Keep in mind that most animals will steer clear of most peppers. In fact, elephants fear the "ghost pepper" and will avoid this plant in the wild. So, if even large herbivores avoid pepper plants, then why do people frequently consume something that would appear to be hazardous? Experts speculate that early man observed parrots and other birds feasting on peppers. These peppers are an important part of a wild bird's diet.

So enter a hungry indigenous American. He sees birds eating from pepper plants and decides to try them. What he doesn't realize is that birds lack taste buds, so the hottest pepper will have no effect on them. The indigenous man takes the first bite... and within milliseconds, he is desperate for water. He manages to swallow some of the pepper. Concluding that it could not get any worse and uncertain of where and when he will get his next meal, he takes a few more bites. But it does get worse, and the man gives up. He decides that hunting wild boar would be preferable. Motivation and starvation set in, and he goes off in search of better hunting.

A few days later, the man's annoying neighbor comes over to brag about how many large, tasty wild boars he has caught. Tired of suffering from neighbor envy, the indigenous man decides to finally one-up his pesky neighbor. He begins to extol the virtues of peppers, describing them as a magical food that is unlike any other— and is even better than wild boar. The neighbor, mesmerized by the story, decides that he must try this new food. The neighbor declares that there must be a feast so that everyone can watch him determine which is better: roasted wild boar or peppers.

Now our hero is in a bit of a bind. He is pretty sure that someone else in the tribe has tried peppers before. If that person warns the neighbor, the jig will be up and the man will be considered a deceiver. The last tribal deceiver was downsized—in other words, chased off.

So our indigenous hero decides that the best thing to do is to disguise the peppers the neighbor will eat. He starts by mashing together the largest peppers that he can find, but the paste is still too recognizable by the telltale seeds and skins. He searches the forest and finds a few wild tomatoes. He mixes cut tomatoes with the pepper paste and finds out that the mix is even hotter than the pepper he ate the other day. It seems that crushing peppers into a paste intensifies the heat. So he throws in some salt and lime juice to preserve the mixture. As an afterthought, he adds some cilantro to mask the color of the robust green chilies.

Tasting the mixture again, he finds that the flavors are interesting, though still spicier than anything he has had before. He then practices bracing himself to take a large mouthful of his new creation. He plans to offer to eat with his unsuspecting neighbor to lull him into taking a huge mouthful of the spicy mixture. He is certain that his neighbor will take the first bite and then beg for water, or better yet, break out in tears, while our hero will remain unfazed.

That night at the feast, the unsuspecting neighbor announces the challenge. The neighbor calls forth our hero to present the peppers. Naturally, the wild boar, which has been smoked and cooked over an open fire, looks far more impressive than the bowl of mashed vegetables, and the feasters laugh. Our hero, always one to take advantage of attention, declares that he is so certain that his dish is better than roast boar that he will eat the pepper concoction along with his neighbor. Then everyone can watch their reaction to each food. The neighbor declares that first they will both taste the roast boar.

Both men simultaneously take a piece of the roast wild boar. At this point, the clouds part, cherubs come out and sing, and both men appear very satisfied. The people at the gathering cheer, and everyone is pretty sure that nothing could be better. When our hero brings out his dish, the neighbor calls for some tortillas to be brought out. Why not make a meal out of this magical concoction, he asks? A bite of magic would not be enough. Our hero is nervous; he prepared himself for just one hot and spicy bite. His neighbor sees the fear in his opponent's eyes and begins to laugh inside. Our hero asks for a drink, and the neighbor jokes loudly to the person standing next to him that he wants to be ready to wash the taste of defeat out as soon as possible.

Two massive tortillas are filled with the pepper mixture. The two combatants raise them to their mouths. They take their first bite and start to chew. Our hero remains resolute and continues chewing. But the neighbor begins to sweat. His face turns red, and he gasps for air. He reaches over to grab our hero's drink, yet the fire in his mouth cannot be quenched. Desperately, he fans his tongue with his hand. When that offers no relief, the neighbor drops his filled tortilla, bolts from his chair, and runs toward the river.

Our hero watches with great glee and continues to munch, gingerly taking small bites. Eventually, the neighbor returns to watch his opponent finishing up. He does not understand what has happened—and how our hero has survived.

The people of the tribe start giggling, and the neighbor senses that somehow he was set up. He is fuming mad, and he wracks his brain to figure out a way to save face. The neighbor calmly walks over and filches the last bite of his opponent's meal. Ready for the worst, he starts to eat it. He's startled—he was certain that our hero must have been eating something bland, but to his surprise, it was just as hot as his. Sweating, he forces himself to finish the tortilla.

Now the neighbor is seriously vexed. How is it possible that his opponent was unfazed by the heat of the pepper mixture? He picks up the tortilla he dropped on the ground earlier and finishes it. The tribe is stunned, and people begin whispering. They decide that the mixture in the tortilla must be better than roast pork—anything so good that one would be willing to eat it off the ground must truly be the best food ever. Others start to come forward to try it. Each person takes a bite, runs away, and comes back a little while later to keep eating. Eventually, a woman puts a tiny bit of the mixture and some pork in a tortilla to make some pretty spectacular tacos. By the end of the event, the pepper dish, now called "salsa picante," is a staple of the tribe. At every celebration thereafter, eating salsa and racing to the river are part of the festivities.

> **Best practice:** Consider the symbolism of the hot pepper in the story. Reflect on who you are more like in the story right now. Do you feel that you were similar to someone else in the story in the past? Might you be like someone in the story in the future?

What does this story tell us? Peer pressure can influence people in groups to do things they wouldn't otherwise do—even things that are not necessarily wise. But in an organization, the power of peer pressure can be harnessed for good, to move the organization forward. The challenge is formalizing cultural peer pressure and directing it in a manner that is structured, organized, and consistent.

Making a Plan for Cultural Change

To use peer pressure to shape an element of culture, you need a plan for change and a method to keep the organization from relapsing back into its old ways. To determine what elements need to change, start by considering the seven elements of organizational culture and how they function in your organization. Then you must consider what the new culture should look like.

Start by writing a brief description of what you'd like the culture to become and which people can leverage such changes. Then consider how the change might look if taken to the extreme. For example, suppose the change your organization is trying to make is to put more emphasis on cross-training. At one extreme, perhaps the organization starts promoting cross-training over current projects, to the point that it is not convenient or practical. Cross-training might become excessive and organizationally disruptive. On the other extreme, a few negative experiences with cross-training could make people less likely to support the initiative. One should also consider the people who would support such an initiative and garner their support to pressure others towards the new program. The more you can do to influence positive feelings and promote positive interactions regarding the change, the more likely it is that the anticipated cultural change will take root.

After considering the possible extremes, build a plan for the cultural shift. The plan does not need to be as detailed as a project plan, but it can be. At a minimum, the plan should address the following:

- Elements of culture that will be affected by the change
- Brief description of the old culture
- Brief description of the new culture
- Timeframe for the change(s)
- Who needs to buy into the change
- What resistance can be expected
- How the resistance can be overcome
- Once the organization has begun to shift, how organizational peer pressure will be applied to keep the momentum
- What will indicate that the change has become a part of the culture
- What will be done to maintain the change as part of the culture.

Rolling Out a Cultural Change

Once the plan for change has been developed, consider how it will be implemented. Most project managers prefer formal rollouts for a new program. There is certainly a benefit to a formal rollout of a cultural shift. If the project manager is comfortable with this approach, then he should move forward in that manner.

Others prefer a less formal rollout. There are two primary advantages of an informal rollout:

- People in the organization will perceive the change as matter of interest, rather than an order. When individuals are required to do things, it becomes work. It stops being fun because deadlines and milestones depend on doing what is required.
- Informal change can be implemented faster by focusing on just the immediate team, rather than the larger organization. When you start by changing just a small group, the change can be replicated throughout the organization. Team members can talk about their experiences regarding the change with others. Positive sharing like this—in other words, peer pressure—can help others to embrace the cultural shift.

Consider these factors when you are trying to determine whether to launch a cultural change formally or informally. Also, keep in mind that an informal launch can evolve into a formal launch; starting small and then changing direction can be an effective approach to getting the change program moving. Building upon small achievements can lead to larger achievements.

Finally, a continuous process that will perpetually sustain the program or shift must be developed. What will help keep the program in existence? One common method is to link the shift to compensation. If cultural improvement is rewarded financially, a greater number of people will try to make a difference to earn this reward. If a certain change is rewarded, such as using a new payroll system, most people will respond positively and will facilitate the change as much as possible. This will not work, however, if the compensation program cannot be changed quickly enough.

Other options include recognition, awards, punishment, and praise. Organizational recognition can help showcase certain achievements. In particular, one should recognize people for exhibiting behaviors that grow the organization. Recognition should be done as publicly as possible to reach the largest number of people. When recognizing people for contributing to organizational growth, craft the recognition as a story. Instead of just stating that Lois, for example, earned the organizational safety award, explain the story behind the decision to give Lois the award. One should offer clear details on what led up to the recognition, rather than just stating a name. Craft an eloquent story to highlight the person and the process, rather than just focusing on the award. Organizations thrive and grow on positive mythos.

CREATING A FLEXIBLE CULTURE

Culture is an artificially created human construct that helps create a sense of order for an organization. It builds a framework that defines the groups within. People want to be differentiated from others; groups need the barriers of differentiation that culture creates in order to feel different and unique. This is particularly important in virtual organizations; differentiation creates a degree of separation between the "us" and the "them," creating a feeling of connection between the virtual team members.

Cultural dynamics also shape what is achievable in organizations. They serve as constructs that limit organizational greatness. Even though each organizational culture is unique, they are all built upon the same elements, and people are always the architects of culture systems.

> **Best practice:** Culture is not static. When you feel too comfortable with the culture of your virtual organization, that is the time at which you should pay closer attention to the culture. Does the culture seems static? Are you doing something to keep the culture from changing?

To build a flexible culture, it is important to look closely at the elements that can change within a culture. In Figure 6-1, we've

Monitoring cultural temperature	Building morale and good feelings about the organization
Communicating effectively	Providing the right tools of communication
Training the team	Offering professional and cultural training
Knowing the market	Learning about your competition in the marketplace
Mentoring employees	Helping build better employees
Emphasizing retention	Promoting from within and helping place people within the organization
Holding employee get-togethers	Encouraging a sense of community
Recognizing and awarding good work	Rewarding good work and success
Performing exit interviews	Learning why people leave the organization, to build a better culture moving forward
Indoctrinating new employees	Training about the culture from the moment an employee starts with the organization

Figure 6-1:   Cultural Elements That Promote Flexibility

focused on nine elements that create and define culture. Focusing efforts on these elements can help create a flexible culture. The more elements you can change, the more the culture will change.

Monitoring Cultural Temperature

Cultural temperature is the overall morale of people in an organization and their feelings about the organization. It can rise and fall, depending on the degree of change. If people feel that the change was communicated well in advance and makes sense, then they will resist the change less. If change is thrust upon people without notice, they will most certainly resist it. Telegraphed change is often better than ambushed change. An organization's cultural temperature will rise and fall with the degree and type of change that is experienced.

One can change an organization's culture by learning what makes people in the organization happy and doing it. Sometimes doing something as small as buying lunch for the group is enough to make morale soar. Learn what engenders positive feelings in your organization, and leverage these things to keep the organization flexible.

Communicating Effectively

Communication is taking steps to better manage and explain happenings in the organization. Good communication and company events help solve problems and help employees understand the organization's culture, while poor communication will weaken the culture and reduce morale. A company that communicates well also is one that will be flexible enough to adjust to what the future brings. People can adjust if they know what is coming.

Training the Team

Training is defined as the refinement of an individual's skills and performance. A positive culture will encourage training and development, while negative cultures avoid offering training, perhaps because they consider it an unnecessary expense. Offering training in professional skills and in the company's culture will keep the organization flexible. The more training people have, the better able they will be to cope with the challenges of their job, and the more they will be willing to go along with changes in the company.

Knowing the Market

The external market is described as the parameters that affect the internal workings of the organization. They can impact morale and decrease organizational productivity. The problem is that these factors may be difficult or impossible to control, such as new government requirements, general loss of faith in the overall market, or competitors' actions. Too often, if the competition is doing something, then the organization must do the same to remain competitive. When the external market demands that the organization change, make it clear that the company is remaining flexible in order to remain competitive, not to add more work.

Mentoring Employees

Through employee mentoring, formal mentors help new employees navigate through the organization. Mentoring is intended to benefit the organization as a whole, too, by creating positive feelings about the culture, increasing employees' fulfillment, and improving employee retention. If an organization does not already have a mentoring program, it should consider starting one. Not only will it help foster organizational flexibility, but it will make individuals more flexible. It is a lot easier to be flexible if you see a leader—your mentor—being flexible.

Emphasizing Retention

Retention emphasis is part of an organization's commitment to its employees. Employees are often concerned about whether their company promotes from within or if it prefers hiring external candidates. A company's retention emphasis will shape employee decisions to remain with a company more than anything else. Salary can be a factor, but if other factors such as employee fulfillment and job satisfaction are equal, employees are more likely to stay than leave.

Related to retention, are long-term employees considered valuable, or are they considered a liability? The treatment of long-term employees will make a difference in how flexible people are willing to be. If long-term employees are rewarded and not punished or forced into retirement, people will want to remain. If experience is valued and achievement is rewarded, people will be more willing to move past their comfort zone for recognition and additional reward.

Holding Employee Get-togethers

Employee gatherings have been identified as a way to create a positive culture. By creating a participatory, "family" atmosphere, organizations can help bring people together as a group or team. A sense of belonging is important because it will help improve the overall cohesiveness of the organization. People want to belong, so the more opportunities you can create to help that feeling along, the better off (and more flexible) the organization will be. Keep in mind that gatherings can be virtual, so don't assume that traditional events like team picnics are necessary if they are not feasible.

Recognizing and Awarding Good Work

Awards and recognition are opportunities to offer acknowledgement for good work and achievement within an organization. If people are being rewarded for good work and achievement, then they will seek out ways to generate more achievement. Improvement leads to achievement, and the more the organization improves, the more flexible the culture must become to facilitate this improvement.

Performing Exit Interviews

Exit interviews do not necessarily have a positive or a negative effect on a culture, but they help organizations gather valuable feedback about why employees leave. This information may help the organization prevent any unfortunate or undesired departures in the future. People often leave places of employment for reasons that the organization itself cannot control. To build a stronger and more flexible culture, it can also help to guide decisions. Specifically, exit interviews can offer insight on any organizational deficiencies driving talent away. If you can find out what is wrong with the culture, you have a better chance at fixing the culture for those that remain.

Indoctrinating New Employees

Indoctrination is the transfer of the organization's culture to employees. Training, such as an initial course to help explain what the company expects, and mentoring are pathways for indoctrination;

however, the term implies a greater immersion into the culture by creating an atmosphere that requires the compliance of those who want to be part of the culture while culling those who are not interested in embracing those virtues. Training the culture, reinforcing the culture, and following the culture will create a stronger culture and, in turn, a stronger virtual project organization.

The Elements of Culture

These elements of culture offer a way to make organizations more flexible to address the future. Every organization must remain vigilant in all of these aspects. A positive culture will support an organization through difficult times, while a negative culture will pull down an organization. Keep in mind that rapid growth can mask the overall culture—when an organization is expanding and projects are plentiful, everything seems to be a lot easier to deal with. When times are tough, many people will depart a negative organization in search of a more positive one. The goal is to build a consistent and flexible culture that will be effective in both good and bad times.

BALANCING DIFFERENT NEEDS

In all organizations, a majority-minority dynamic will arise at times. A smaller group will feel as if a larger group is trying to enact an unfair change. When this happens, a rift will develop between the groups. This is, of course, not the ideal situation for a virtual (or any) organization. The good news is that there are methods to either avoid or mitigate this kind of situation. These strategies include continuous improvement teams, increased communication, training, and change awareness.

Continuous Improvement Teams

A continuous improvement team is a cross-departmental team formed to strengthen a project or organization by improving communication and creating a sense of ownership. Ownership, in turn, creates a sense of community. A continuous improvement team must have a balance between people of the perceived majority and those of the perceived minority. An imbalanced team will be perceived as a vehicle for changing one group or the other. Consider that seats in the U.S. House of Representatives are apportioned by population, while each state, regardless of size, gets two seats in the U.S. Senate. Each house of Congress balances out the other. If the Senate did not exist, the needs of the smaller states would be ignored.

A continuous improvement team should address the following action items:

- Creating a place to gather employee suggestions
- Offering feedback and following up on those suggestions and other issues
- Expanding and creating new organizational rituals
- Implementing or improving training
- Enhancing the mentoring system, if one exists, and creating a mentoring system if one does not exist.

A continuous improvement team can also foster improved communication through symbols and stories (e.g., the hot pepper story told earlier), to improve internal communications for projecting the organization's long-term vision, for example. Offering a metaphor like the Phoenix Project conjures up a vision of a bird rising up from the ashes. Images or symbols can be used to communicate quite effectively and quickly. They also can become a rallying point, which will help to instill a sense of pride in the company. Just as the U.S. flag can be a rallying point for military personnel in times of conflict, or the way a battle cry like *Remember the Alamo* inspired Texans, create a symbol that can be equally inspiring.

Communication

Communication channels that allow the majority and the minority to engage in two-way communication are ideal. Two-way communication enables management to hear *and* respond to employees. One possible way to accomplish this is an open lunch forum where employees may speak directly to upper management about issues of concern. This can be done by video conference or by phone in a virtual environment.

Sometimes, employees need to be able to communicate open and honestly while remaining anonymous. It is possible to create a two-way system of communication that preserves the anonymity of the employee. This method, if properly implemented, can also help management manage the office grapevine or rumor mill because it lets employees ask questions and air concerns with management without fear of retribution, and it gives management a chance to address these concerns. If employees do not believe that management is being honest with them, they will turn to the rumor mill as their sole source of information. Because the rumor mill may or may not have valid information, fear, uncertainty, and doubt will run rampant throughout the organization. Clearly, this is detrimental to the organization and will reinforce feelings of majority versus minority.

In a virtual environment, a high-tech approach to confidential communication should be considered. Options might include a dedicated website, an electronic bulletin board system, or an 800 number. These systems work best in a technology-based culture, where everyone has access to the system and can easily make contributions. Employees will ignore systems that are inconvenient to use, attributing their ineffectiveness to management's lack of understanding of their needs.

> **Best practice:** Consider that everyone involved in a virtual project organization will not speak English as their primary language. Consider multiple forms of communication, such as emails, phone calls, video chat, instant messaging, and even face-to-face contact to ensure that everyone understands the message.

Training

Training should be required whenever rapid changes occur that were triggered by the growth of the organization. Too often, employees receive only cursory or sporadic training when organizations expand. Insufficient training yields dissatisfied employees who will perpetuate the mistakes and the poor habits of the past. The "ineffectiveness" of the training then becomes an excuse to further restrict the training and leads to a feeling of failure within the organization. Inadequate training, like inadequate communication, also intensifies feelings of majority versus minority.

Implementing Change

How an organization chooses to implement its ideas often deter-mines the overall success of the changes it makes. If the organization does not create a valid implementation plan that has various check-points at which feedback is given, it will be difficult to determine if the changes are effective. Also, without this kind of process, there will be groups made up of those who know about the change and those who do not know about the change, and, in turn, this will create the kind of majority-minority situation that organizations must avoid.

To discourage the development of a majority-minority situation, project managers must adhere to the following ideal process:

- Establish definite periods and milestones for a change project so that the organization can chart its progress—and know when it is done.

- Establish key success factors that indicate whether the organization has achieved the desired results.

- Be prepared for change. In any complex process with an extended duration, the environment will change over time, and the leader must document these changes and circulate the information to all the stakeholders.

- Call a review meeting with all the stakeholders. This review, perhaps one year after the change is implemented, can measure whether the desired changes were made.

Additionally, there should be periodic "success meetings," at which the organization's leaders talk about various scenarios that are conducive to heroes and winners. Leaders can give motivational speeches or pep talks to talk up the project and the organization. People want to feel like they are part of a successful project, and highlighting the challenges and successes is one way to make peo-ple want to be part of the project. People from all strata of the organization should attend these meetings. Without buy-in from all levels, any organizational change is doomed to failure, and the organization will be more susceptible to problems caused by majority-minority tension.

Best practice: Consider that different countries have different cultural norms and behaviors. Learn more about the cultures of people in your virtual project organization and keep their norms in mind during a project. Respecting other cultures will help everyone embrace the project and its leader.

Change makers must understand that organizational change is like planting a tree. The process takes time, and the tree must be nurtured. Change has to start at the root source, which is the top of the leadership chart. The head of the organization must lead the planting and nurturing of culture changes. Then he or she must support the implementation of those changes by actively participating in decisions related to the changes. To use another metaphor, shifting a culture is like trying to cross a busy freeway—it is possible, but it must be done with care.

As discussed, better communication, greater creativity, systems of reward and recognition, training, and mentoring are all important to a healthy culture. If continuous attention is paid to organizational culture, the organization will do better in good times and in bad. Keep in mind that when times are good, project managers and organizations tend to ignore culture because they are busy, but when times are tough, they struggle with cultural issues. It is not that the cultural issues were not there before; the problems were always there, but during the lean times, people notice them more and worry more about them. Addressing cultural issues during the good times will help avoid these kinds of organizational energy saps during the bad times.

Project managers must ensure that all team members are delivering results consistent with the organizational culture and values (Bolman and Deal 2003; Schein 2004). No one should operate outside, or above, the culture. Teams that try to distance themselves from a cultural change will not achieve lasting success. The key to success is working together with the change.

Chapter 7

COMMUNICATION

It's evident that "organizations aren't the visible, tangible, obvious places which they used to be" (Handy 1997, p. 378). Communication distribution systems—in other words, the technologies people use to communicate—are now an important force in effective internal and external organizational communications. As technology continues to improve and becomes less expensive to implement, virtual organizations will become the norm.

Effective personal and organizational communication is critically important in a virtual project management organization (Cascio 2000; Duarte and Snyder 2006; Scholz 1998). It is also complex, because organizations are not the traditional brick-and-mortar places that they were in the past (Handy 1997, p. 378). On the advice of organizational theorists, organizations of the past often continuously monitored team members; now, many organizations realize, or will realize, that it is not necessary to "own all the people needed to get the work done, let alone have them where they can see them" (Handy 1997, p. 378). Ideally, the continuous monitoring of project team members would no longer be required, because in a VPMO, individuals own their processes, and they need to be left alone to get their jobs done. Virtual project organizations must shift from the traditional structure of single-person leadership to a focus on individuals' ability to lead and manage themselves (Cascio 2000).

Some people believe that virtual communication will lead to chaos. Technology allows people to access information instantly, and people enjoy many different communication options. In today's business world, face-to-face communication and even telephone calls are less common because other means and methods of communication are available and convenient. It is a lot easier to send a quick email at 9:00 p.m. to a colleague than to pick up the phone to give her a quick update on a project.

SPECIAL CONSIDERATIONS IN A VPMO

A traditional team communicates directly through face-to-face contact. Body language, other visual cues, and tone underscore meaning (Duarte and Snyder 2006, p. 142). Virtual teams, of course, must rely on indirect communication in the form of telephone calls, emails, faxes, and other technologically based methods (Duarte and Snyder 2006). Personal contact will always be essential, but it does not require being physically proximate. Continuous contact, more than proximity, is what bonds people together. The virtual project management office can operate with less face-to-face communication, although direct contact is still the best way to facilitate effective communication.

Imagine what it would be like to be on a submarine that has no contact with anyone outside of the selected few on board. What kind of relationship might these individuals have with the outside world? How connected would these people feel after a few months without contact? Think of the people on a virtual team as being on that submarine. Each person has a job to do and a mission to accomplish, but without some access to information from the outside world, they may feel detached and alone. The job of the project manager is to be the bridge for these people to the outside world. He or she must make those people feel connected to the project in such a way that they feel valued and trusted.

> **Best practice:** Designate time each week to reach out to the more distant members of the virtual project management organization. Give peripheral stakeholders a short, personal update on the project. After the update, ask what they think about the project. (Keep in mind that the view of the earth from Pluto is vastly different from the view of the earth from the moon.)

Even though "people can work together connected only by phone, fax, or E-mail" (Handy 1997, p. 378), the virtual project manager must realize that technology cannot make up for poor or lacking communication. Experts agree that the virtual environment requires that communication be clearer and more concise. Reach also is important. Email, blogs, and texts can be important tools, but they have to reach people at all levels of the organization if they are to be effective. Hence, the project manager must learn not only to communicate more, but also to improve the distribution of information.

Figure 7-1 details some of the reasons organizational communication either works or doesn't. Ineffective communication may be either too intense or not intense enough in terms of the volume, or amount, of communication; its substance; its type; or its quality.

Communication				
INTENSITY	Volume	Substance	Types	Quality
HIGH	Information overload	Too technical	Too many types of communication are being used	Information is too detailed for general information
MEDIUM	The amount of information strikes a good balance	There is a good balance of technical and social information	Face and phone time are well balanced with electronic communication	There is a good balance of detailed information regarding the project
LOW	Too little	Too social	Face and phone time, as well as electronic communication, are insufficient	Not enough details for general information

Figure 7-1:   Evaluating the Quality of Communication

Real communication is about distributing important information. Project managers should not simply act like messengers. Simply passing along information via email is not real communication; this does nothing to ensure comprehension, nor does it foster connections between people. Project managers should use information as a way to build a rapport with others—in other words, to create trust. It does not take much time or effort to add a few explanatory words to an email. Make communication important and make it count.

Best practice: Everyone in the VPMO must remember that communication is very important. Make communication effective at every opportunity. Shun just passing along data, and embrace passing along tangible positive experiences. Will we remember those who liked us the most, or will we remember those who sent us the most emails?

CHALLENGES

Technology is the link between the individual and the virtual project management office, requiring the organization to carry the burden of a dispersed information technology infrastructure to maintain its remote sites. The virtual organization's dependence on technology can lead to technical challenges that may exacerbate communication issues (Cascio 2000; Karl 1999) caused by the lack of robust personal contact that comes from day-to-day physical proximity and interaction.

Working across great distances may require working with people in different time zones, from different countries and cultures, and who speak different languages (Karl 1999). Roberts, Kossek, and Ozeki (1998) found that executives dealing with virtual projects were challenged by having to disseminate innovative, "state of the art knowledge and practices" throughout the organization while trying to overcome the fact that although English was the language of business for all the companies within the study, English was not the native language of everyone working on the projects.

Best practice: Respect the schedules of stakeholders in different time zones and schedule meetings as fairly as possible.

People in virtual project management organizations may feel isolated because they do not have the same opportunities for casual social interaction around the coffee maker or water cooler that people in traditional companies do. These social interactions include, on the positive side, the passing on of vital organization information and information on others' activities, and on the negative side, the passing on of rumors about the organization. Both types of communication are necessary, as even seemingly negative interactions create an atmosphere of connectedness to the organization.

To avoid isolation, team leaders must harness technology to facilitate contact and keep individuals in the loop (O'Connor 2000; Cascio 2000). To encourage good communication, the virtual project manager should ensure that all team members have compatible technology. The virtual project also should quickly organize databases that allow sharing and learning. Duarte and Snyder (2006) recommend establishing "shared lessons, databases, knowledge repositories, and chat rooms" (p. 17) to enhance virtual teams' learning and communication opportunities.

COMMUNICATING WITH STAKEHOLDERS

The first and most important element of communication is actually doing it. There are many reasons for the failure of organizational communication, but one of the simplest reasons is that communication is not happening often enough. Companies spend billions of dollars each year on communication technology—only for people to act as if they do not have time to put together a meaningful, accurate project status report (yet they seem to have time to post tweets or update their status on Facebook). One possible reason is that it is more fun and interesting to chat away with friends than to talk with people whom one is less familiar with or worse, with someone that one is afraid of.

People spend many hours with others at work, yet our colleagues can be the hardest people to communicate with. Why is this? One reason is that usually, more is at stake in work communications. Friends rarely beat us up for missing deadlines or not always having exact change to cover lunch. But it's difficult for a project manager to report to clients that a project is running late or over budget. One cannot make everyone in the project a friend, but at least one can make their interactions with others interesting and productive. The less reluctant people are to communicate with each other, the more communication will actually happen.

Virtual project management leaders need to make sure they are communicating with all of the relevant individuals on a project. To determine who the stakeholders for a given project are—in other words, who needs to know what is going on—start by doing a communication assessment. Use Figure 7-2, which lists categories of stakeholders with whom you may need to communicate, as a guide.

Stakeholder Group	Composition
Senior management	Major shareholders, executives, the Board
Management	All impacted functional areas within the organization
Employees	All impacted individuals within the organization
Impacted business units	All impacted related companies or divisions
Contractors	All involved suppliers and consultants
Industry	Competition and other companies
Communities	Local and state organizations who are impacted
Commercial interests	Banks and related financial institutions
Government institutions	International, national, state, local institutions
Regulators	Any overseeing regulating body
Environmental interests	Any environmental agency, such as EPA

Figure 7-2:   Common Project Stakeholders

Once the stakeholders have been identified, determine whether the relationship between your organization and the stakeholder is contractual, organizational, or informational. If there is a contractual relationship, the individuals and groups involved need at a minimum certain economic and milestone-related data. Communication with this group should include detailed information about contract milestones, contract changes, contract payments, and the project timeline (schedule). Uncertain whether your organization has a contractual relationship with a stakeholder? Just follow the money. For example, even though a subcontractor of your supplier is not given a check with your company logo, if you follow the money trail, there is no doubt that there is a contractual type of relationship between your organization and the subcontractor.

There is an organizational relationship if there is some kind of organizational connection between the project manager and the other individual or department. Usually these kinds of relationships are obvious because they are shown on an organizational chart. Follow the lines on the organizational chart—if there is a connection, then the relationship is organizational. If this is the case, you need to offer the same information you would if there were a contractual relationship, but your updates should also include any greater implications of the project as it relates to the company. For example, if it is necessary to complete your project before another project can start, you must make sure that stakeholders know this so that they're aware of the ramifications of a delay in your project schedule. In short, you must explain the bigger picture so that others will understand the situation.

If the relationship is not contractual or organizational, it should be informational. In an informational relationship, updates should be kept as short as possible. Use them to highlight the project team's achievements. It is important to keep groups with whom you have an informational relationship apprised of progress, but you do not want to pass along too many details. Details create questions, and questions create more questions, and this will result in your spending more time on updating these stakeholders than is necessary. Project managers who spend too much time communicating updates and general information are at risk of falling into the virtual project management information time trap, discussed later in this chapter.

Best practice: Consider mapping the lines of communication for all of a project's stakeholders—in other words, study their interactions and how they overlap. The web of communication is very important in a virtual project management organization because of the value of open communication. Understanding how communication operates within a team is important for project success.

ORGANIZATIONAL STRUCTURE AND COMMUNICATION

Anyone who has spent time in an organization is familiar with a standard organizational chart. Lines and boxes connect people together in a manner that shows the reporting structure of the organization. However, an organizational chart does little to show the actual communication structure of the organization. In the practical world, few organizations are rigid and structured enough to have clear lines of direct communication such as those seen on an organizational chart.

Because the lines of communications may be blurred, in most organizations individuals piece together information to create the big picture. The rumor mill is often a good source of information. There are always individuals who are so connected they learn things sooner than others. Find out who these organizational listeners are and ask for their perspective. A virtual project management office may spend a lot of money and time communicating the organizational vision, but that might not be the most effective manner to communicate other information. So it is important that individuals learn how to assimilate all of the incoming data and create a view of the organization that is consistent and accurate. If people have an alternative source of information, then the official channels might not be as effective.

In the VPMO, it is also important that individuals and leaders come together to create creative, independent groups that have individual and specific purposes. One may want to fault the organization for not providing a road map for doing so, but the reality is that these kinds of connections need to develop naturally. If they are forced, communication may become stilted, and weak communication is one reason that people resist change.

Best practice: There should be a way for feedback to be passed along to the highest levels of the company without any filtering layers. Project managers do not need to report to top management, but there must be a mechanism for project managers to be heard. Consider asking the CEO to meet informally with different project managers to gather their thoughts on ways the organization can improve.

Think of an organization like an onion instead of like a hierarchical grouping of lines and boxes. The sections of an onion are so tightly pressed together that the onion appears to be a solid ball, but each layer is really connected only at the base. The layers are similar to each other, but each layer grows at a different angle and the layers are different sizes so that they can fit into one another to create what looks and feels like a solid sphere from the outside. This onion metaphor helps us better understand how individuals in an organization are connected. An individual is like a layer of the onion, connected to the whole, but completely different from the other layers. It is critically important for the leadership in a VPMO to recognize these different human constructs. Leaders who do are better equipped to move their organization from homeostasis towards a particular goal.

People want to retain their individuality without losing their identity, and they also want to be part of a greater whole. On the surface, this appears to be a paradox. People in virtual project management organizations must learn to work in conjunction with one another, yet each member of the team can and should make his or her own bold contributions to projects. Individuals can achieve a sense of connection to the projects they work on by integrating part of themselves into their work. A clothing designer, architect, or artist gives a little of herself with every piece of work; everyone wants to have that same sense of creation. Once a project team member has done his part of the work, he must pass the baton along to someone else, who will then add her own perspective to the project in progress.

Consider creating, developing, or evolving flexible and open systems of communication that will be responsive to new situations. Organizations that will be successful in the future are those that are tightly integrated without being codependent. In the past, organizations strove to be like an apple, a homogenous mass, completely solid, with no room for sudden change. Now organizations must strive to be more like an onion, with layers that fit together neatly, to remain resilient and flexible without losing sight of the whole or the individual.

> **Best practice:** Reflect on the fact that organizations should be more like an onion than an apple. Consider how the structure of the organization might affect organizational communication.

> **Best practice:** Always consider how you communicate with others in the organization. If people are fairly close by, consider walking down the hall to talk with them rather than just sending an email. Visit vendor locations to see how they operate and observe their processes. You can learn more from talking face-to-face, so do your best to make personal contact whenever possible.

COPING WITH NEGATIVE COMMUNICATION

A three-step process (see Figure 7-3) will help those working in virtual environments cope with negative communication. The process can also be used in traditional office environments, but it is applied differently. It is important to recognize the difference and to apply the correct techniques to the situation to avoid more communication problems in the future.

Identify   >>>   **Address**   >>>   **Follow up**

Figure 7-3:   The Process of Correcting Negative Communication

First, you have to identify whether the negative communication is a face-to-face issue or a virtual issue. There are critical differences in the dynamics between traditional, collocated teams and virtual teams. A traditional team communicates directly, through face-to-face contact. People use the communication style they are most comfortable with to express dissatisfaction; people who like to vent in person are unlikely to send a negative email. Negative in-person communication should be responded to in person. Matching your response to the perpetrator's style of communication will help ensure that the message is received.

What if the negativity is communicated virtually? Virtual teams, of course, rely on indirect communication in the form of telephone calls, emails, faxes, and other technologically based methods (Furst et al. 2004, p. 7). Keep in mind that the perpetrator of the negative communication may blame technology for creating a misunderstanding. As part of the process of addressing the negative communication, you must educate the individual in virtual etiquette and make it clear to him that future communication should be clearer and more concise. Avoid allowing him to blame technology, unless there is some real technical hindrance.

Furthermore, you need to follow up regarding negative communication. If no one follows up, you won't have an opportunity to correct the process. Clarify what was negative about the communication, and replace it with something positive. The more you can eliminate negative communication, the better off the organization will be.

> **Best practice:** Monitor the effectiveness of the identify > address > follow-up process when dealing with a negative communication issue, and determine what can be done better the next time.

Research indicates that virtual project managers, like brick-and-mortar ones, face conflict during the team forming and storming stages of the Tuckman model. Other research has emphasized that in the virtual environment, trust is essential for effective management. It can be reasonably concluded that a competent PM will gain the trust of team members (Duarte and Snyder 2006). Duarte and Snyder (2006) report that competent project managers are those who effectively communicate with customers and teams and set high expectations. Because the forming and storming stages are the first two phases of a project team's life, the team has not yet been able to establish the necessary trust with the project manager. It may be helpful for the project manager to meet face-to-face (electronically or traditionally) with the team to demonstrate her competence, which should increase the trust quotient.

> **Best practice:** Coping with negative communication is always challenging. Address people's negativity quickly, concisely, and consistently. Doing so will help you create a positive culture.

DELIVERING CLEAR, DIRECT, AND CROSS-CULTURAL INFORMATION

The leadership of the organization is responsible for making sure that important information is delivered in a timely, clear, direct manner. Good communication is self-reinforcing because people will remember and use the content of the message. A message that is confusing or full of obscure technical jargon is not effective. Clear communication accurately communicates a message. It must be complete and devoid of vague references that could be misinterpreted. Direct communication clearly explains the message and the expectations for the person receiving the message. It is also focused on the topic at hand.

Best practice: Consider how many times you communicate with others in one day. How many of those communications could accurately be described as clear? What can you do in the future to make your communications clearer?

If the audience for a message is international, leadership must determine if the message will be effective cross-culturally. Clear communication is understood by everyone, regardless of their culture or native language. A message going to an international audience must be even better crafted than one that is sent to your immediate team. Just translating your marketing materials is not sufficient; the message must be communicated with the same level of clarity and passion as it is in English. If a message is vague and unclear or not meaningful to recipients from other cultures, you may need to create a new message that works well internationally. Keep in mind that culturally specific references, for example to American football or certain U.S. celebrities, will probably mean little to, and so fall flat with, international audiences. To get additional perspectives on an important project message or announcement before sending it out, consider asking multiple colleagues to review the message. Better yet, to ensure that the message is clear, consider asking reviewers from multiple countries for their feedback.

Best practice: When communicating internationally, consider using different examples to make the point clearer. Try to insert more relevant examples that will resonate better with individuals from other nations. Instead of examples pertaining to baseball, consider using soccer examples.

DELEGATING AND RELEGATING COMMUNICATION

Providing information often leads to questions, which lead to answers, which lead to more questions or a desire for even more information. On top of this, the nature of the virtual project management organization creates a need for more information. Because people in virtual environments lack the kind of water cooler social networking opportunities they would have in brick-and-mortar businesses, they also may not be getting as much information as they would in traditional offices. They may rely on the virtual project manager to answer questions and research more information, which takes time—time that virtual project managers should be spending on managing the project. These project managers may find themselves in what we call the virtual project management information time trap, illustrated in Figure 7-4.

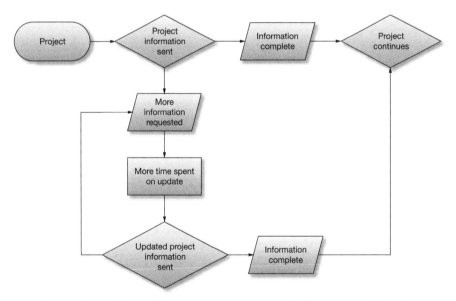

Figure 7-4:   Virtual Project Management Information Time Trap

A project manager who finds himself in this time trap must immediately regroup and consider the kind of information that is being distributed, either officially or unofficially, that is causing stakeholders to have so many questions. Excessive demands for more information indicate that the project manager is not providing enough regular updates, the project is starting to spiral out of control, or others in the organization doubt that the project manager will be able to complete the project.

Work needs to be done before one can communicate about it, so if the project manager is spending too much time on communication with stakeholders, he needs to review his process of communication. Communication should be the final step of the project process, after all of the process steps have occurred. The communication process is a way of taking credit for milestones and achievements. If one is spending too much time on the final link in the chain, one needs to find a way to make more work happen.

Best practice: Have you been caught in the virtual project management information time trap or seen someone who was? What was done to improve the situation?

To avoid the virtual project management information time trap or to get out of it, the project manager must follow a process of delegation and relegation. Here, delegation is the process of asking someone else to handle some of the communication regarding the project. Relegation is a way to better compartmentalize requests for information and to more efficiently communicate information and expectations about the information.

Delegation

Project updates should be a shared responsibility, not just something to be completed by the project manager. Once the reporting and informational requirements (framework) of the project information to be tracked have been determined, then the virtual project manager needs to decide who is responsible for gathering up the details.

When a project is being planned, the project manager should consider appointing a project historian. This is not a full-time position, nor does one person have to stay in the position for the life of the project. The project historian should ask everyone for informational updates about the project, and she should also gather information on what individuals and groups have done for the project. If stakeholders feel that they have the right to ask questions about a project, then they should be asked what they are doing to support the project. It's natural for stakeholders to ask questions and voice concerns, but they should also be held accountable for their actions related to the project.

The project historian is a better person than the project manager to ask stakeholders what they are doing in support of a project, because if the project manager asks this kind of question, stakeholders may perceive it as annoying or confrontational. During the conversation, the project historian can use peer pressure in a positive way by talking about what other stakeholders are doing for the project. If you've ever had to raise funds for charitable organizations, you know that telling prospective donors that others have donated to the cause can help push them to donate. Stakeholder peer pressure can be an effective way to help gain more support for the project.

> **Best practice:** Assign the project historian not only to chronicle the project, but also to create a repository of information that can be reviewed at the end of the project during a lessons-learned session. Subcontractors and consultants also should provide progress updates to be included in the repository of project information. This information can also be used to develop future projects of a similar nature.

Relegation

A virtual project manager needs to shape stakeholders' expectations by relegating communication to the most appropriate time. The project manager should not drop everything to answer an email from a stakeholder. Even if you think that dashing off an answer will resolve the question quickly, it is better to wait. Quick responses rarely result in closure. Keep in mind the unwritten organizational axiom that emails that are answered quickly will always result in a follow-up question. Supposedly quick answers become time wasters when they create or do not resolve uncertainty.

SOURCES OF RISK

Uncertainty about what someone wants or is trying to say could be attributable to any of the five basic sources of risk related to communication, as given by Garrett (2007):

- A lack of understanding
- Shortcomings of language or interpretation
- People's behavior
- Haste
- Deception.

A Lack of Understanding

It is critical that communication regarding requirements and deliverables be understood by the recipient. Not all stakeholders will have the same level of knowledge about the project, so certain information, abbreviations, acronyms, or technical jargon might be confusing. A project manager must keep his audience in mind when crafting messages. Communication cannot succeed if the audience does not fully understand it.

Shortcomings of Language or Interpretation

Human language is complex, and verbal communication usually has elements of tone and body language that help us decode other's meaning and intention. When people communicate virtually, body language cannot help convey their meaning, so the messages they send could be perceived as incomplete or confusing. Written communication can be interpreted in different ways by different people.

On international projects, keep in mind that translations are not always as clear as one would expect. Additionally, even if the project language of choice is English, team members may interact with people whose primary language is not English.

In all virtual communications, keep in mind that the message conveyed must be consistent (Garrett 2007), and you should attempt to communicate that message in several different ways, such as by email, phone, or face-to-face interaction—to reinforce the message, action items, and deadlines.

People's Behavior

When communication is inconsistent or lacking, oftentimes the involved parties will behave in a manner that is inconsistent with the expectations placed on them. If expectations are confusing, individuals will modify their actions based on what they believe to be the expectations. It is common for people to move towards easier guidelines or to behave in a manner that is more aligned with their own agenda than with the goals and objectives of the project. If they believe they have a choice, most people will choose the easier road and follow their own preferences. These are not always incongruent with the goals of the project, if the organization has strong values, but it will certainly not be the most efficient path to project success.

Haste

Haste often leads to undesirable results. Rushing to meet a deadline has a way of increasing the number of mistakes, reducing quality, and causing rework. The pressure to complete a project on time or to attain certain milestones can cause individuals to disregard safety, policy, or procedures in order to achieve the expected goal (Garrett 2007). The pressures of haste can often lead to dangerous situations that can impact a project, or in extreme cases, an entire company or industry. Consider BP's haste to reach an oil deposit with the Deepwater Horizon. Safety and other protocols were ignored in order to strike oil as fast as possible. Haste, in this case, resulted in the death of 11 people and led to the worst environmental disaster in recent history.

Think about this situation when you are in a hurry on a project. If a virtual project manager feels pressured by an encroaching deadline to cut corners, she should consider how haste could result in a very negative situation for the virtual project management office. If someone has barely enough time to finish the tasks at hand, that person will have little time to communicate his or her status to others. This loss of communication time can seriously impact a project if stakeholders have to turn to less reliable, secondary sources for information.

Deception

Whenever money changes hands, there is the possibility that one party will attempt to deceive another for potential gain. Intentional treachery may be to blame, but deception is usually not intentional; sometimes it is a result of a misunderstanding of the requirements of the project. For example, new system implementations most commonly fail because the system provider unintentionally deceived the client. The supplier believed its solution would fit the client's needs, but it became apparent during implementation that the system was never capable of achieving the client's requirements (Garrett 2007).

Note that communication risk is not limited to generally risky or complex projects. It's important to understand risks associated with communication and work to identify and mitigate them, as risk reduction can increase an organization's longevity, among other benefits. So how can a project manager do her part to reduce communication risk? She must learn to modify her behavior in the future. In the future, instead of firing off a quick email response, she should wait and consider a more careful answer that has definite closure as its goal. Specifically, the project manager should:

- Consider the list of communication risks above when crafting the response (and any time she needs to communicate about a project).

- Set a response time for the answer (consider waiting 24 hours).

- Close by asking the recipient what he is doing to support the project. This encourages him to provide information instead of asking more questions. The recipient's answers can be included in the next project update.

- Forward these responses (or pass them along to the project historian) to other stakeholders as appropriate. They will show the stakeholders how others are supporting the project. Evidence of stakeholder support will generate more interest than basic updates on budget and schedule would. Showing how others are supporting the project demonstrates its positive effects.

ELEMENTS OF COMMUNICATION

Once an organization is committed to developing or expanding its virtual project management organization, it must come to grips with the fact that moving forward, almost all of the organization's communication will be done virtually. This does not mean that the organization should consider virtual communication to be the only form of communication, but it must understand that it will be the primary way people in the VPMO reach out to stake-holders. Some might see this as a hindrance to the organization, but a real understanding of virtual communication will allow the organization to leverage its strengths.

Virtual organizations must take advantage of online communication, which is more adaptive than people may realize. It offers a richness of information that was previously not believed to be possible. In the past, virtual organizations were limited to sharing information via simple text interfaces because of cost, bandwidth, and technology restrictions. Hence, online communication was brief, disjointed, and one-sided. Although technology has expanded to offer greater flexibility in communication, it appears that the typical means of communication continues to be the simple memo. Email has made memos easier to circulate, but, in the end, an email is still a type of memo.

In the past, hard-copy memos were the only manner of managing organizational degrees. Hard-copy memos would be handed out to the relevant people. If they had questions, they would walk down the hall to discuss the matter with others. Because a memo was static and might not provide answers for every possible scenario, it was only a piece of the communication relationship. In today's virtual organization, people do not have same familiarity with one another, so most of the time, documents (usually electronic) must stand on their own. Few people in virtual organizations frequently reach out to discuss information they receive because they assume that it should need no further explanation.

> **Best practice:** No memo ever changed the world. Even the Emancipation Proclamation, the document that forever freed slaves in the states that were in rebellion against the United States, did not change the world. It was the action of people after the document was signed that changed the world. Remember that memos are just pieces of paper; it is the actions of people that actually effect change.

A memo, or any piece of written communication, is composed of two primary elements: a degree of visuals and a degree of voice. The secondary element, which is often unrecognized, is the human interaction (HI) between individuals affected by the memo. In a traditional business environment, people can pass on information via visuals and voice (V&V) as well as through human interaction. The primary vehicle of information transfer in written communication is based on visuals (e.g., words, displays, charts). Visuals can be adapted to video or, in some cases, voice recordings.

The ratio of V&V and HI is not 50/50; it is driven by people's individual communication style. Keep in mind that there are no requirements for the human interaction element; however, an organizational leader would be considered particularly ineffective if he or she did not allow people to ask questions regarding new processes, policies, or procedures.

There is no magic behind an effective memo or communication. Whether a communication effort works is based on how the material is presented and how well it is absorbed by the intended audience. On a virtual project, this will likely be done online. Technology and a little creativity can help you produce something more interesting and memorable than a static memo, such as videos or podcasts.

The human interaction element includes asking questions and answering them and solving problems. Interaction helps reinforce the message being presented. In a traditional organization, where all parties are available for an impromptu discussion or clarification, this can happen in person. HI is also possible in a virtual environment, and it is important, as it will improve the virtual communication process. Of course, HI needs to be enabled by technology on a virtual project, and sufficient training and support are needed to make virtual HI successful (Runyon 2010). If an organization is committed to regular virtual interaction, it must invest in technology, including video conferencing software or even a video studio.

Best practice: How people interact is often more important than the information that is exchanged. How can tone be used in virtual communication to enhance or clarify a message?

Best practice: Many people can talk for hours, so it is hard to believe that so many of them are actually poor communicators. In terms of communication style, people tend to be similar to birds. Birds sing to attract a mate, mark territory, or share information. Their songs are audible to a wide range of animals, including humans. The bird is unconcerned about who hears its song (if a bird was worried about predators, it certainly would not give its location away by singing). People, like birds, can broadcast information about their lives without always revealing their true feelings. People tend to hold back more information than animals. If a bird feels threatened, it will attack or flee. If a person feels threatened, he can attack, flee, panic, hide, or lie. This variety of reactions makes human communication difficult to understand.

Bees communicate in a substantially different manner. They cannot vocalize, so they must use a complex dance (and possibly scent) to communicate with their brethren. This kind of communication is very specific and substantive. The bee needs to make sure that the hive is aware of a food source or of potential danger lurking in the distance. Bees' communication is never concealed, and their direct communication is important for the survival of the hive. Directed communication like this is the kind that is effective in a project environment.

Most communication in an organization is general and wholly unrelated to the project at hand. The minority of communication is actually productive. The key to effective communication on a project is getting people to spend a little more time communicating like a bee and less like a bird.

Communication must be an integral part of the VPMO. The organizational structure of the VPMO must allow for communications to flow to and from the VPMO and up and down the chain of command. The VPMO leaders should consider themselves advocates for all aspects of project management. To do this, they must be adept and effective oral and written communicators.

In a virtual world, the written word is sacrosanct, and the virtual project relies heavily on the written word. The VPMO can provide a valuable offering to the project community by helping the project teams communicate effectively. The VPMO should provide training on the different lines of communication, the implications of a relative lack of face-to-face communication, body language, culture, communicating with stakeholders in the virtual environment, and many other aspects of virtual project management.

The VPMO staff may also provide hints to the virtual project manager on ways to assess loneliness. Remember, by nature humans are social creatures. The virtual project manager has to make sure that team members don't become isolated.

Part III

BEST PRACTICES

All organizations must have processes and procedures based on best practices to enhance their chances of success. Figure III-1 outlines the next three chapters, each of which covers a set of best practices and provides tools, templates, and suggestions that might be implemented in a VPMO.

Implementation and Expansion Tools
Virtual Implementation and Expansion Tools
PMO Implementation and Expansion Tools
System Implementation and Expansion Tools
Process Implementation and Expansion Tools
Procedural Implementation and Expansion Tools

Evaluation Tools
Virtual Evaluation Tools
Risk and Investment Evaluation Tools
System Evaluation Tools

| Process Evaluation Tools |
| Trust and Culture Evaluation Tools |

| **Lessons Learned and Best Practices** |
| Best Practices: Autonomy and Trust |
| Best Practices from PMOs |
| Best Practices from Virtual Organizations |

Figure III-1:   VPMO Tools, Lessons Learned, and Best Practices

Chapter 8

IMPLEMENTATION AND EXPANSION TOOLS

This chapter includes course templates that support the implementation of a VPMO as well as tools that the VPMO can use to analyze organizational change, flexibility, and trust. The course templates can be used in two different situations: for a full implementation of a new VPMO or for an expansion of an existing VPMO. Keep in mind that multiple observations over time are necessary to establish a true understanding of an organization. A single observation at a single point in time can often skew the results, so one negative (or positive) result is not necessarily meaningful.

VIRTUAL IMPLEMENTATION AND EXPANSION TOOLS

Formal group training is recommended when implementing virtual work. Figure 8-1 is a sample outline and schedule for a workshop held before the establishment of a virtual project management office. Figure 8-2 consists of similar materials for a workshop an organization might hold as it plans to expand its use of virtual elements.

Workshop: Creating a Virtual Project Management Office

Learning Objectives

To create a virtual organization: *Define the vision for the targeted organization*

To explain the process of becoming a virtual organization

Goals of the Seminar

Incremental transition or dynamic transition? *To be defined by the targeted organization*

Dealing with setbacks: *Define the organization's resources and alternatives*

Coping with failure: *Define alternative strategy, if available*

Monitoring the change: *Define how this will be done*

Leveraging the virtual organization: *Explain the benefits to the organization and the individual*

Seminar Outline

   I.   Introduction
        a. Define virtual organization
        b. Discuss virtual teams
        c. Dismiss myths about virtual organization/virtual teams

  II.   Virtual organization
        a. Shortcomings
        b. Benefits

 III.   Virtual team
        a. Shortcomings
        b. Benefits

  IV.   Why go virtual?
        a. Traditional organizational structure
        b. Virtual organizational structure
        c. Hybrid organizational structure

   V.   Change (movement)
        a. Incremental change
        b. Dynamic change

  VI.   Change management
        a. Migrating to a virtual organization
        b. Dealing with virtual setbacks
        c. Coping with failures

VII.   Leadership
    a. Monitoring change
    b. Leading change

VIII.   Future and Benefits
    a. Leverage the change
    b. Leverage the virtual teams
    c. Plan future path of organizational development

Schedule for a One-Day Seminar

(6.5 hours total instructional time; one hour for lunch, two 15-minute breaks)

Time	Topic
9:00 a.m.–10:00 a.m.	Introduction to virtual organizations (VO) Introduction to virtual teams (VT) Define *teams* Discuss myths about VO/VT Review benefits of VO/VT Review shortcomings of VO/VT Review VO/VT
15-minute break	
10:15 a.m.–11:30 a.m.	Discuss virtual leadership Discuss virtual culture Why go virtual? Why remain traditional? Discuss VO Discuss traditional organizations Discuss hybrid organizations Review VO

Time	Topic
11:30 a.m.–12:30 p.m.	Leadership in the VO/VT Discussion of culture Discuss leading change Discuss monitoring change Review leadership, culture, and change
Lunch 12:30 p.m.–1:30 p.m.	
1:30 p.m.–2:30 p.m.	Migrating to a VO Making the migration a project Creating a project plan Establishing milestones Review the migration plan
2:30 p.m.–3:00 p.m.	Dealing with virtual setbacks Coping with failures Strategies for success in the VO Review successes and failures
3:00 p.m.–3:45 p.m.	Review a case of a VO transition
15-minute break	
4:00 p.m.–5:00 p.m.	Leveraging VO/ VT How to plan for the future of the organization Making VO the dominant culture Wrap-up and final questions and answers

Figure 8-1: Outline and Schedule for a Workshop on the Creation of a Virtual Project Management Office

Workshop: Increasing Virtual Deployment

Learning Objectives

To increase deployment of a virtual organization: *Define the vision for the targeted organization*

To explain the process of becoming more virtual

Goals of the Seminar

Incremental transition or dynamic transition? *To be defined by the targeted organization*

Dealing with setbacks: *Define the organization's resources and alternatives*

Coping with failure: *Define alternative strategy, if available*

Monitoring the change: *Define how this will be done*

Leveraging the virtual organization: *Explain the benefits to the organization and the individual*

Seminar Outline

    I.   Introduction
- a. Define virtual organization
- b. Discuss virtual teams
- c. Dismiss myths about virtual organization/virtual teams

   II.   Virtual organization and virtual teams
- a. Shortcomings
- b. Benefits

 III.   Why is going more virtual necessary?
- a. Traditional organizational structure
- b. Virtual organizational structure
- c. Hybrid organizational structure
- d. Ideal future structure

 IV.   Change management
- a. Incremental or dynamic change
- b. Migrating to a more virtual organization

   c. Sharing best virtual practices across the organization

   d. Dealing with virtual setbacks

   e. Coping with failures

V. Leadership

   a. Monitoring change

   b. Leading change

VI. Future and benefits

   a. Leveraging and monitoring existing virtual elements

   b. Leveraging and monitoring increases in virtual teams

   c. Planning the future path of organizational development

Schedule for a One-Day Seminar

(6.5 hours total instructional time; one hour for lunch, two 15-minute breaks)

Time	Topic
9:00 a.m.–10:00 a.m.	Discussion about virtual organizations (VO)
	Discussion about virtual teams (VT)
	Define teams within the organization
	Discuss myths about VO/VT
	Review benefits of VO/VT
	Review shortcomings of VO/VT
	Review VO/VT
	Discuss how expansion will benefit the individual and the organization
15-minute break	

Time	Topic
10:15 a.m.–11:30 a.m.	Discuss virtual leadership Discuss virtual culture Why go more virtual? Why not remain traditional? Discuss VO Discuss traditional organizations Discuss hybrid organizations Review virtual organizations Discuss the ideal virtual organization for the company
11:30 a.m.–12:30 p.m.	Leadership in the VO/VT Discuss culture Discuss leading change Discuss monitoring change Review leadership, culture, and change
Lunch 12:30 p.m.–1:30 p.m.	
1:30 p.m.–2:30 p.m.	Moving toward to a greater use of virtual tools and elements Making this expansion a project Creating a project plan Establishing milestones Review the plan to increase virtual elements Generate agreement and buy-in for the plan

Time	Topic
2:30 p.m.–3:00 p.m.	Dealing with virtual setbacks Coping with failures Strategies for success in the VO Review successes and failures
3:00 p.m.–3:45 p.m.	Review a case of increased virtual use Review the competition's increased use of virtual methods
15-minute break	
4:00 p.m.–5:00 p.m.	Discuss best practices for virtual organizations Leveraging VO/VT more for the future How to plan for the future of the organization Making virtual the dominant organizational force Wrap-up and final questions and answers

Figure 8-2:   Outline and Schedule for an Increased Virtual Deployment Workshop

Best practice: The virtual project management office must regularly offer and promote individual training. Make sure that people continue to train by requiring them to participate in some kind of learning experience every six months. If the competition continues to train regularly and people in your organization do not, then your organization will fall behind.

PMO IMPLEMENTATION AND EXPANSION TOOLS

In this section, we will review two tools for evaluating the current organization with regard to the branding of change and to training. Both branding and training should be very important to the PMO and the VPMO because there will always be a need to understand and monitor change and to train staff. World-class organizations have continuous training programs that allow individuals to grow within their role and within the organization. Programs like these benefit PMOs as well as VPMOs.

As discussed in Chapter 5, it is important to brand change. The change branding review checklist in Figure 8-3 can be used when contemplating the implementation or expansion of a VPMO to help ensure that all aspects and dimensions of the brand are identified in the process. Many organizations incorrectly believe that all that is needed to brand something is to give it a catchy name and an interesting logo. Although those elements can be important, one must understand that the more thought that goes into the brand, the stronger it will be.

Figure 8-3 can also be used to develop a plan for a potential brand of change. It might not be possible to fully develop the brand at the outset, but you should be able to complete a strong framework and come up with ideas for addressing any areas that are incomplete. The checklist reviews seven core elements discussed in Chapter 5, and it also focuses on the elements necessary to develop a plan for the brand of change.

Keep these organizational elements in mind and include any additional comments at the end in the notes section. This tool is used to better define in short sound bites the important elements of the brand and how the change will impact the organization. Use this to better focus the ideas and efforts related to the brand. Note that this tool can be used in conjunction with several other tools in this book that address change and culture.

The second tool is a training checklist for the VPMO. The organization must create a training plan. Toney states, "[T]he best practices project organization has a personalized development and training program based on identification of skills and competencies needed by the individual or group" (2002, p. 241). Successful

Name of the Brand: _____

(Write a brief description of the elements of the brand and how the brand will assist and support the change that it represents.)

1. Identify and quantify the costs of branding the change.	
2. Map out the schedule for the change. Write down the important milestones for the brand.	
3. Identify the champion and any other stakeholders who will own this change. List everyone who will be impacted—both positively and negatively—by the VPMO.	
4. Describe the purpose and desired results of this brand.	
5. Identify how this brand will impact the culture of the VPMO.	
6. Identify how this brand will impact communication in the VPMO.	

7. Explain the metaphor or icon associated with the brand.	
NOTES:	

Figure 8-3: Brand Review Checklist

organizations rely heavily on training to maintain the standards of the organization. If a robust training plan is not developed or training is not continuous, then the VPMO will not succeed. It will slowly decline, as fewer and fewer trained project managers will be available to lead projects. An organization does not become a VPMO by accident, nor does it remain a VPMO by accident.

There are two types of VPMO organizational structures:

- Everyone in the organization is considered a project manager, and everyone will need some type of project management training. These organizations are based on project generalization.

- Specific individuals are designated as project managers, and teams have been identified as project teams. These project managers and team members will go from project to project within the organization. These organizations are based on project specialization.

Once the type of organization has been established, it's time to identify the training that must be established to maintain the organization. Training types include ongoing project management training (introductory and advanced), communications training, leadership training, cultural training, as well as initial indoctrination training. Figure 8-4 offers a framework for documenting a training plan.

Training Topic: _____

(Write a brief description of the training topic.*)

1. Identify and quantify the costs of the training.	
2. Map out the schedule for the training.	
3. Identify the champion who will own this training.	
4. Describe the purpose and desired results of this training.	
5. Identify how this training will impact the culture of the VPMO.	
6. Identify how this brand will impact communication in the VPMO.	
7. Explain the name of the brand and the identity of the brand (change).	

*Training topics can include training in technologies that support communications, systems that support communications, processes that support communications, and anything that supports the expansion of virtual elements within the organization.

Figure 8-4:   Project Management Training Checklist

See Chapters 10 and 13 for additional material on training.

SYSTEM IMPLEMENTATION AND EXPANSION TOOLS

VPMOs are composed of many different systems, including communication systems, human resources systems, project management systems, and more. When planning to implement a VPMO or considering expanding an existing VPMO, one needs to understand the entire organization as a whole. Examining a single system or approach is not sufficient. Specifically, it's essential to understand the level of flexibility to successfully implement or expand a VPMO.

This section has two integrated tools, the VPMO flexibility audit (Figure 8-5) and the VPMO flexibility audit progress chart (Figure 8-6), which will allow for formal monitoring and charting of the organization's flexibility over time.

The VPMO flexibility audit examines ten different organizational elements, but it is an aggregate assessment of flexibility. Since a given person may not be able to assess all of the elements of flexibility, the process allows for a single score to represent the level of flexibility. If a best practice listed on the audit is one the organization uses, the person doing the audit documents the details of how the organization has implemented the best practice. If the organization does not follow a given best practice, the auditor leaves the area blank. At the end, the auditor should calculate the score, which will range from 1 to 10. If the auditor is not certain enough about a given element to assess it, she should assign a prorated score to each element that she did assess. For example, if she

Use this tool to determine the level of flexibility of the current organizational culture. Conduct this audit periodically to determine if the organization is becoming more or less flexible. How often and in what way is the organization addressing these elements?

Cultural temperature: morale, "feeling" of organization	
Communication tool used	
Professional and cultural training	
External market: knowledge of the competition	
Employee mentoring: How is this helping to build better employees?	
Retention emphasis: Is the organization promoting from within?	
Employee gatherings: creating a sense of community	
Awards and recognition: Award and recognize good work	

Exit interviews: Do you find out why people leave?	
Indoctrinations: initial training about the culture	

OVERALL RATING (1 to 10 scale):_____

NOTES:

Figure 8-5:   VPMO Flexibility Audit

was able to review only five elements, she should allot two points to each element so that the total possible score will still be 10.

A flexibility audit should be conducted periodically, preferably weekly, so that one can review the results over time, typically over a one-month period. This will allow a fuller understanding of the organization. If time is of the essence, consider doing the flexibility audit daily for several days.

The second tool, the VPMO flexibility audit progress chart, offers a method for creating a bar chart that can be used to track readiness for implementing or expanding a VPMO. By examining elements of flexibility at multiple points in time and charting them together, one can readily see variations in the organization's flexibility and hence its readiness.

An average score of 7 or more over a period of four separate, time-spaced audits indicates that the organization is flexible and would readily embrace a VPMO concept or the expansion of an

When reviewing the results of this chart over time, the best result is a consistently high rating. If you see either an increase or decrease in the rating of more than one point, the flexibility of the organization might be situational. Regardless, a low value of flexibility will indicate that the organization is not very adaptable.

10				
9.5				
9				
8.5				
8				
7.5				
7				
6.5				
6				
5.5				
5				
4.5				
4				
3.5				
3				
2.5				
2				
1.5				
1				
.5				
Date: _____	Date: _____	Date: _____	Date: _____	

Figure 8-6:   VPMO Flexibility Audit Progress Chart

existing VPMO. An average score of 4 or less over a period of four separate, time-spaced audits indicates that the organization is not flexible and would actively resist a VPMO.

If scores vary by more than one full point between audits, then the organization may be situationally flexible. For example, an organization might become more flexible if a certain supervisor is on vacation and is replaced by a different supervisor for a period of time. If audit scores suggest that the organization is situationally flexible, then it is a good idea to look a little deeper to discover the true source of this variation.

PROCESS IMPLEMENTATION AND EXPANSION TOOLS

The two tools in this section can help you assess and understand how people in your organization cope with change. Coping with, or adapting to, change is organizationally essential because organizations are constantly changing. Because change is recognized as such a dynamic force, much research and time has been devoted to its study.

People and groups may rely on very different coping mechanisms. The coping with change audit tool (Figure 8-7) offers a method to grade an organization's or individual's ability to cope with change in a positive manner. Negative coping tactics like complaining can be damaging to the organization. If the individual or organization copes with change in a negative manner, that individual or group should receive a lower score. In most cases, one should drop the score by one full grade (A drops to B, B drops to C). The auditor should keep in mind that each section should be assessed objectively and separately. A poor grade in one quadrant should not affect the individual's or group's other grades.

Strategies for Coping with Change

Consider the four strategies for coping with change: responsibility, planning, speed, and contingency. Review how effective the VPMO has been in coping with change, and issue a letter grade from A to F for each strategy. Write a brief description of what can be done better in the future. If you rate yourself an A, justify that grade.

Communication grade: _____	Areas for improvement:
Planning grade: _____	Areas for improvement:
Speed grade: _____	Areas for improvement:
Contingency grade: _____	Areas for improvement:

NOTES:

Figure 8-7: VPMO Coping with Change Audit

The second tool, Figure 8-8, is the VPMO coping with change progress review. This tool can be used to catalog and evaluate the grades for the organization or individual over time. The audit is short enough that it could be done daily for a period of time, or observations could be done over a much longer period of time. By examining multiple points in time and reviewing them en masse, one can readily see how variable individuals' or the organization's ability to cope with change can be.

Responsibility	Date	Evaluation				
		A	B	C	D	F

Planning	Date	Evaluation				
		A	B	C	D	F

Speed	Date	Evaluation				
		A	B	C	D	F

Contingency	Date	Evaluation				
		A	B	C	D	F

Figure 8-8: VPMO Coping with Change Progress Review

An organization that copes well with change should have consistent grades. Even consistently low grades suggest that the organization is coping with change in a regular, if not ideal, manner. If the coping process is good (consistently high grades), then you just need to support the process as it is. If grades are consistently low, then the process is in need of modification.

The problem is when grades are both high and low. When there is a pattern of inconsistent grades, then the organization is coping with change randomly. This means that most mechanisms are ad hoc and the organization is making temporary fixes in order to get by. This is the worst possible finding because you will need to dig a lot deeper in order to find out what exactly is wrong. At this point, it is helpful to find out what is working (indicated by the high grades) and then try to apply that learning to correct the systems that are not working (indicated by the low grades). You must be sure that the organization has consistently high grades before trying to implement a VPMO or expanding the organization's virtual capabilities. As with the flexibility audit, you need to make sure that the coping mechanisms are working well to ensure that the organization will adapt to the changes that a VPMO will bring.

PROCEDURAL IMPLEMENTATION AND EXPANSION TOOLS

When a VPMO is established or expanded, many new and different procedures will be necessary. It's important that the organization be a trusting, honest one before it attempts to become more virtual. In an organization where trust is weak, procedures are often implemented because the organization wants to protect itself from individuals trying to take advantage of the organization. People may assume that new procedures are a response to someone doing something wrong. In these organizations, new procedures will create negative rumors. In one organization, a new employee hotline was established to fulfill a Sarbanes-Oxley requirement. When the hotline was announced, several managers were offended by the new policy and promptly dubbed it the "snitch line." Clearly, there was not a lot of trust in that organization because people assumed that the new procedure was designed to encourage employees to rat out their colleagues.

The trust audit checklist in Figure 8-9 will help ascertain the level of trust in an organization. This checklist is based on the pillars of trust discussed in Chapter 4 (see Figures 4-2 and 4-3).

> **Best practice:** Consider administering the short trust survey (see Figure 4-1) and completing the trust audit at the same time to get additional feedback on trust in the organization.

Because it can be difficult to define trust, it is best to take a multifaceted approach to assessing it, to mitigate bias and misinterpretations. Each pillar of trust is represented on the checklist. The auditor reviews and grades each of the elements that make up trust separately.

Issue a letter grade from A to F for each element of trust, and write a brief description of how it is expressed in the VPMO. Make sure to describe how these elements of trust support the VPMO.	
Communication grade: _____	Description:
Predictability grade: _____	Description:
Honesty grade: _____	Description:
Credibility grade: _____	Description:
Passion grade: _____	Description:
Courage grade: _____	Description:
Competency grade: _____	Description:
Integrity grade: _____	Description:
NOTES:	

Figure 8-9: VPMO Trust Audit Checklist

Grade the extent to which each element of trust is expressed in the VPMO according to the following standard:

- A is awarded when trust levels are outstanding within the VPMO. Trust indicators are clearly identifiable and commonly observed and applied.

- B is awarded when trust levels are very good within the VPMO. Trust indicators are identifiable and consistently applied.

- C is awarded when trust levels are average within the VPMO. Trust indicators are regularly identifiable but not consistently applied.

- D is awarded when trust levels are below average within the VPMO. Trust indicators are not typically identifiable or applied.

- F is awarded when trust levels are not found within the VPMO.

When conducting the audit, refer back to Chapter 4 to make sure that your grading is consistent with the definitions of the various pillars of trust. This will ensure the consistency of the findings. Consistency of interpretation will allow for consistency of grading, which will allow this tool to be used by different people in multiple locations with similar results.

Figure 8-10 offers a method for assessing the progress of trust in the VPMO over time.

Communication	Date	Evaluation				
		A	B	C	D	F

Predictability	Date	Evaluation				
		A	B	C	D	F

Honesty	Date	Evaluation				
		A	B	C	D	F

Credibility	Date	Evaluation				
		A	B	C	D	F

Passion	Date	Evaluation				
		A	B	C	D	F

Courage	Date	Evaluation				
		A	B	C	D	F

Competency	Date	Evaluation				
		A	B	C	D	F

Integrity	Date	Evaluation				
		A	B	C	D	F

Figure 8-10: VPMO Trust Progress Review

The trust progress review allows for the tracking of the grades generated through the use of the VPMO trust audit checklist. You should conduct the audit several times over a period of time, then average the grades for all of the aspects of trust, which would then in turn generate a final grade—just like grades in school. If a large number of grades have been generated or if the grades vary considerably, determining a final average grade can be difficult. In that case, convert the grades to numbers and take an average of all the grades. An A would equate to 4 points, a B would equate to 3 points, a C would equate to 2 points, a D would equate to 1 point, and an F would equate to 0 points. The average would then convert back to a letter grade, using the same scale.

Alternatively, you can determine average grades for each aspect of trust. This method is particularly helpful if the overall score is low; individual averages will indicate which aspects of trust are missing or less present in the organization, which will help you figure out what to focus on to improve trust.

This chapter provides several tools, including checklists and reviews, that you can use when planning to implement or expand a VPMO. These easy-to-use tools can be used to monitor various elements of the organization and to identify problems or potential problems. The tools are designed to help direct VPMO leaders toward areas of improvement within an organization. They can help leaders focus their efforts for change and improvement without having to spend a lot of money on consultants.

Remember that practice and consistency is important when using any tool. The tools in chapter will be more effective in identifying problems in the organization if they are used regularly. Several of them were designed to be used over a period of time in order to generate more consistent results. When a tool is used only once, it may suggest that an outlier is the norm (because it will be assumed that whatever was observed is normal), so consider using any tool a few times in order to achieve a normal or typical result.

Chapter 9

EVALUATION TOOLS

This chapter offers various tools for evaluating the VPMO or its progress toward becoming more virtual.

VIRTUAL EVALUATION TOOLS

In this section, we will review two tools: one that can be used to evaluate the organization's current use of virtual elements, and one that can be used as a follow-up to monitor the progress of the organization as it becomes more virtual.

Figure 9-1 is a tool for self-assessing the virtual organization. It will help you determine what elements of virtual operations exist within your organization and may increase your understanding of what is necessary for successful virtual operations. You will answer five questions about virtual communication, your organization's support of virtual communication, and the presence of technology available to support a virtual environment. The virtual organization self-assessment should take no more than 20 minutes.

Expect to spend about 15–20 minutes on this self-assessment. Respond to the items as quickly and accurately as possible. Write down the answers that come to you first, rather than dwelling on the items.	
Process Questions	**Response**
Process One Reflect upon the current project management organization. Do you regularly communicate virtually with your organization?	

Process Two Reflect upon the current project management organization. Do you regularly communicate virtually with your project team?	
Process Three Reflect upon the current project management organization. Do you regularly communicate virtually with others as a typical means of communication?	
Process Four If virtual communication is a primary means of communication, what is being done to support virtual communication within the organization?	
Process Five Reflect upon the level of technology available for the organization and for the project team and consider whether there is sufficient technology to support 100-percent effective interaction. If there is any doubt, consider what needs to be done for the organization to become completely virtual.	

Figure 9-1: Virtual Organization Self-Assessment

Once you have completed the assessment, consider what you and your organization are and are not doing in support of virtual work.

- If certain virtual elements are present, consider how they should be implemented or improved in the future.
- If certain virtual elements are sometimes present, how can the organization take greater advantage of them in the future?
- If virtual elements are present in some areas but not others, consider how the organization can be realigned so that its use or implementation of virtual elements is more consistent.

This tool should serve as a platform to create an action plan for improving the level of virtual elements within an evolving VPMO. The second tool, the virtual improvement assessment process (see Figure 9-2), can be used as a follow-up to the virtual organization self-assessment or on its own. The second tool asks deeper and more probing questions about the VPMO that are intended to indicate areas the organization should focus on to better leverage its VPMO or make it more efficient. This assessment should take no more than 30 minutes.

Expect to spend about 20–30 minutes on this self-assessment. Respond to the items as quickly and accurately as possible. Write down the answers that come to you first, rather than dwelling on the items.	
Process Questions	**Response**
Process One Is the technology needed to support an increase in virtual activities available within the project management office? If so, answer yes; if no, write what is needed to achieve this goal.	
Process Two Is there a change management process to support moving towards more virtual activity within the project management office? If so, answer yes; if no, write what is needed to achieve this goal.	
Process Three Is it evident who could lead the organization towards more virtual activity? If so, write their names down. If no, write what might be needed to achieve this goal.	
Process Four Who could be a stakeholder of a project to expand the project management office's virtual capabilities? List the groups and individuals that would be involved, and note the change makers, takers, and breakers.	

Process Five	
Think about how you could brand the expansion of the project management office's virtual capabilities. What would you name the project? Consider any other requirements that must be met for the organization to become completely virtual.	

Figure 9-2: Virtual Improvement Assessment

The first three questions require a response of yes or no in order to force the respondent to make a firm judgment. If the response to a question is yes, then typically little or no action is required. If the answer is no, then that element needs further attention. The purpose of the tool is to indicate which virtual elements need improvement before the organization implements or expands its VPMO.

RISK AND INVESTMENT EVALUATION TOOLS

The two tools discussed in this section can be used to evaluate how the organization handles risk and return on investment. There will always be individuals who want to understand why the organization should invest in a VPMO and the risks that accompany implementing or evolving a VPMO.

An important first step when developing or expanding a VPMO is to review and evaluate the associated risk factors. Figure 9-3 provides questions on trust, communication, culture, and stakeholders and champions that relate to VPMO implementation.

Consider the associated risk factors and ask how they would impact the implementation at a VPMO. There is no perfect way to implement a VPMO, but one must understand and address the organizational risks to have an effective transition to a VPMO.	
Trust: Does trust exist in the organization? How important is it to the organization? How would trust support a VPMO?	

Communication: How effective is communication in the organization? What aspects of communication are present, and how would they support a VPMO?	
Culture: How effective is the culture in assisting with change in the organization? What aspects of culture are present, and how would they support a VPMO?	
Stakeholders and Champions: Are stakeholders present and supportive of the VPMO? Has a champion been identified for the transition to a VPMO?	

Figure 9-3: VPMO Risk Factor Assessment

The evaluator should answer the questions based on his personal observations and experiences. This instrument might need to be completed over time because the evaluator might not have the answers to all of the questions immediately. It is recommended that the evaluator do some research before answering the questions, but this should not take more than a few days. If the spaces provided are not large enough to include all of the gathered information, use additional blank sheets to complete the questions. The evaluator's answers to the questions should indicate the possible risks associated with developing a VPMO in that organization. The answers should also suggest key people that should be involved in the VPMO moving forward.

The second tool, the virtual project management return on investment review (see Figure 9-4), is useful on its own or as a follow-up to the risk factor evaluation.

Costs	→	Savings
VPMO training: communication, technology, systems, processes	→	Time savings from implementation of the VPMO

VPMO equipment: communication, infrastructure, telecommunications systems, processes	→	Asset savings from implementation of the VPMO
VPMO connectivity: Internet, telecommunications systems	→	Savings on infrastructure and office space
VPMO recognition programs: employee recognition, team recognition, project recognition, organizational recognition	→	Process improvement drives savings by increasing productivity, reducing implementation costs, and reducing organizational waste

Figure 9-4:   VPMO Return on Investment Review

The tool identifies four typical costs and four typical areas of savings that come from a VPMO. It includes blank spaces where the reviewer can identify other costs and savings from her own organization's VPMO. Keep in mind that although any VPMO will operate under certain principles, many unique factors and configurations need to be considered when contemplating costs and savings. A VPMO that is operating in multiple countries in many different time zones will certainly be different from a VPMO that has three offices in one state.

The tool in Figure 9-4 is designed only to identify the various cost risk factors. It does not offer a means for capturing or quantifying the value assigned to or associated with each risk. The reason for this is that many organizations have their own internal rates of return and risk-value assignment, so rather than try to encompass all those variables, this tool simply identifies risks that need to be considered. After completing this exercise, it is recommended that the reviewer develop her own valuation of the various costs and savings associated with the risks she has discovered. This will allow her to calculate out a true return on investment for virtual elements in her organization.

SYSTEM EVALUATION TOOLS

This section covers two tools: the level of success evaluation and the level of culture evaluation. Both tools offer methods for identifying factors that may affect key organizational systems. In many organizations, people do not realize that the way systems interact is just as important as the individual systems.

The levels of project success evaluation (Figure 9-5) can be used to determine the successful and less successful elements of a given project.

Success Level	Project Elements	Degree of Certainty	Description of Success Level
Level 6			The project is a big winner, and it has a lot of support from the organization. People want to be affiliated with the project because of its positive impact.
Level 5			The project is a winner and has some support from the organization. People are interested in it because of its positive impact.
Level 4			The project looks like a winner and has some support from the organization. People are asking about it because of its positive impact.
Level 3			The project looks like a loser and has little support from the organization. People haven't given up, however, and some are still trying to rescue the project.

Level 2			The project is a loser, and there is little support from the organization. Some people still want to help, but most are trying to distance themselves from the project at every opportunity.
Level 1			The project is a big loser, and there is little support from the organization. People are trying to distance themselves from the project at every opportunity because they are concerned about their careers.
Categorize the elements of a project by the level of success they have achieved. Remember that too much success or failure may conceal issues on a project. If most of or all the elements of a project are successful, problems may still be hiding behind that success.			

Figure 9-5: Levels of Project Success Evaluation

Success can have an impact on all systems—and that impact is not necessarily positive. On a successful project, problems are less likely to surface, giving the appearance that everything is operating smoothly, even if it is not. It is a fact of human nature that when times are good, smaller problems tend to be overlooked and pushed under the rug. The problem with this is that once the success fades, problems will surface from apparently nowhere. It's particularly important in a VPMO to identify hidden problems because there are fewer visible signs of problems and opportunities for observation. The VPMO must be vigilant during the good times as well as the bad. The level of success tool can help the leader determine if too much success or too much failure on a project is causing larger issues to remain hidden.

When using the level of success tool, it is most important to review the elements that lie at the extremes. Extreme failure and extreme success can hide organizational concerns or issues.

Elements placed at levels 1, 2, 5, and 6 should be reviewed further to determine if success or failure is causing individuals to hide or avoid discussing larger issues.

As emphasized earlier, good communication is essential in the VPMO, so it is not productive for people to become quiet. Good times and good reviews can make people quiet. If the project is going well and people are receiving accolades, it is hard for individuals to bring up anything that might tarnish the perception of success. Often, people ignore issues they shouldn't. This can become a problem: these issues build, and eventually larger issues are ignored, jeopardizing the earlier success of the project.

Projects in crisis or projects on the brink also can make people quiet. If a project is behind schedule, over budget, or both, people are compelled to avoid discussion about the project's problems, forcing the issues underground. This problem can worsen as more and more project issues go unaddressed, creating a downward spiral. The less people know about the project's problems, the less that people can help, and in turn, the more problems that develop.

The levels of culture evaluation (Figure 9-6) is an assessment of the level at which the VPMO's culture is functioning. It can be used effectively to gauge how strongly people identify with the organizational culture. Refer to Chapter 6 for more information on the elements of culture.

Cultural Level	Cultural Elements	Keyword	Description of Cultural Level
Level 6		Harmony	Very high innovation and risk taking
			Very high attention to detail
			Very high outcome, people, team orientation
			Very high aggressiveness
			Very high stability

Level 5		Constructive Conflict	High innovation and risk taking
			High attention to detail
			High outcome, people, team orientation
			High aggressiveness
			High stability
Level 4		Understanding	Mid innovation and risk taking
			Mid attention to detail
			Mid outcome, people, team orientation
			Mid aggressiveness
			Mid stability
Level 3		Respect	Mid to low innovation and risk taking
			Mid to low attention to detail
			Mid to low outcome, people, team orientation
			Mid to low aggressiveness
			Mid to low stability
Level 2		Trust	Low innovation and risk taking
			Low attention to detail
			Low outcome, people, team orientation
			Low aggressiveness
			Low stability

Level 1		Conflict	Very low innovation and risk taking
			Very low attention to detail
			Very low outcome, people, team orientation
			Very low aggressiveness
			Very low stability

Review the project and list the different elements of culture that best describe the cultural level. Consider that a project could have several elements at different levels. If you find that most or all cultural elements on a project are at a high level, project team members are working together well; if you find that most or all the cultural elements on a project are at a low level, the project needs strengthening of the core elements of culture.

Figure 9-6:   Levels of Culture Evaluation

If you use the tool to determine how strongly a project team identifies with the culture, the evaluation also will reveal how individuals are implementing various systems in their area of work. If people are cooperating and working together, then one would expect the systems in the organization to be running smoothly. If people are not cooperating and working together well, further review is needed to determine what might be the problem. Keep in mind that the culture of an organization should hold it together during good times and bad times, so monitoring culture is a good way to monitor the cohesiveness of the VPMO.

The tool also can be used to assess a specific person's alignment with the VPMO's culture. This assessment is particularly effective in determining who might not support the organizational culture.

We see, then, that the tool can also be used at two levels to examine the total organizational system. One can start by examining the project group; if the review is not entirely favorable, then one can drill down and start examining each person on the team.

Once the individuals who have the weakest identification with the culture have been identified, they can be coached, which will help them become more fully supportive of the culture. The tool will not help correct what might be the root cause of weak alignment with the VPMO's culture, but it certainly will indicate whether the team (or individual) is supportive of the culture.

The tools in Figures 9-5 and 9-6 are independent, but they can be used together if one is concerned about the culture of the project or the entire VPMO. Keep in mind that one might find variations by site. If results are across the board, consider looking at a smaller group, a subgroup, or even at the individual level.

PROCESS EVALUATION TOOLS

This section covers two tools used to evaluate processes in the VPMO: a VPMO change assessment register and a virtual technology and communications assessment. Both tools review processes that are critical to the VPMO.

It is important to determine the level of organizational resistance toward any new or proposed change in a VPMO because change is inevitable and necessary in the virtual environment. The VPMO change assessment register (Figure 9-7) is a worksheet that can be used to track the relative influence of people involved in a change and how vocal they are. This tool should be used to determine the impact that individuals will have on any given change.

Start the assessment by identifying a single change to be made in the organization. Next, consider all the individuals who might be involved, directly or indirectly. Categorize these people as best you can as change makers, change breakers, or change takers. (See Chapter 5 for definitions of these terms.) After identifying each person as a change maker, change breaker, or change taker, determine on a scale of 1 to 3 how influential or vocal the individual is. A score of 3 indicates that the person is influential and vocal; a 2 indicates that the person is either influential or vocal; and a 1 indicates that the person is neither particularly influential nor vocal. Enter each person's name in the relevant column. For example, write an influential, vocal change maker's name in the third column from the left.

	Maker 1	Maker 2	Maker 3	Breaker 1	Breaker 2	Breaker 3	Taker 1	Taker 2	Taker 3
1	Name	Name	Name	Name	Name	Name	Name	Name	Name
2	Name	Name	Name	Name	Name	Name	Name	Name	Name
3	Name	Name	Name	Name	Name	Name	Name	Name	Name
4	Name	Name	Name	Name	Name	Name	Name	Name	Name
5	Name	Name	Name	Name	Name	Name	Name	Name	Name
6	Name	Name	Name	Name	Name	Name	Name	Name	Name
7	Name	Name	Name	Name	Name	Name	Name	Name	Name
8	Name	Name	Name	Name	Name	Name	Name	Name	Name
Type Total									
Score Total	Multiply type by one and enter total	Multiply type by two and enter total	Multiply type by three and enter total	Multiply type by one and enter total	Multiply type by two and enter total	Multiply type by three and enter total	Multiply type by one and enter total	Multiply type by two and enter total	Multiply type by three and enter total

Total value of all change makers: _____

Total value of all change breakers: _____

Total value of all change takers: _____

Figure 9-7: VPMO Change Assessment Register

Once you have entered the names in the correct columns, tabulate the number of names in each column and multiply the total of each column by 1, 2, or 3 (depending on the number at the top of the column). Then total the value of the change makers, change breakers, and change takers. If the value of the change makers is greater, add the value of the change takers to the value of the change makers. If the value of the change breakers is greater, add the value of the change takers to the value of the change breakers. If the values of the change makers and change breakers are equal, then ignore the value of the change takers.

Then, subtract the value of the change breakers from the value of the change makers. If the value is positive, then the force of the change should allow the change to proceed. If the value is zero or negative, then the force of the change is not strong.

Note that the absolute value of this total indicates the strength for or against the change. A high positive number indicates strong support; a high negative number suggests strong opposition. If this is a new change, and this exercise does not indicate significant support, the leader should work with the stakeholders classified as change breakers to educate and influence those who are not supportive. If the change has been proposed but not implemented, and support is lacking or opposition is strong, again, the leader should educate and influence unsupportive stakeholders before proceeding with the change.

The tool shown in Figure 9-8 can be used to review and evaluate the level of technology, communications, and leadership within a VPMO. It is designed to be used at the site or group level only. The matrix lists indicators of high, medium, and low levels of technological sophistication, communication facility, and leadership in an organization. This tool is a quick assessment that is designed to indicate the level at which the VPMO is operating on these three dimensions; it is not designed to identify specific software, hardware, or technology issues. In short, it is best used to determine whether basic VPMO requirements are being met.

The organization should be given high marks only if it has achieved 95 percent or greater compliance in an area, which means that the VPMO's facility in an area must reach everyone or almost everyone in the VPMO. If a VPMO site does not earn high marks in all three areas, then further review using other tools must be done to determine the specific issues that exist.

Level	Technology	Communications	Leadership
High – 95% or greater	• Technology is available to everyone. • Everyone is trained. • Everyone is operating on the same version. • Everyone is proficient. • Everyone is using software and systems that are compatible.	• Communication is highly prevalent. • Many types of communication are in common use. • People are proficient and effective communicators.	• Leaders are available to individuals within the organization. • Leaders are highly proficient and highly effective. • There is a strong leadership presence. • Leadership is valued and respected.
Medium – 0% to 95%	• Technology is available to almost everyone. • Most people are trained. • Most people are operating on the same version. • Most people are proficient. • Most people are using software and systems that are compatible.	• Communication is generally present. • Several types of communication are in common use. • Most people are proficient and effective communicators.	• Leaders are usually available to individuals within the organization. • Leaders are mostly proficient and effective. • There is some leadership presence. • Most leaders are valued and respected.

Low – less than 80%	• Technology is available to few people. • Few people are trained. • Few people are operating on the same version. • Few people are proficient. • Few people are using software and systems that are compatible.	• Communication is not present or prevalent. • Few types of communication are in common use. • Few people are proficient and effective communicators.	• Leaders are usually not available to individuals within the organization. • Leaders are not proficient or effective. • There is weak or no leadership presence. • Leaders are generally ignored.
Rank	HIGH MEDIUM LOW	HIGH MEDIUM LOW	HIGH MEDIUM LOW

Figure 9-8: Virtual Technology, Communication, and Leadership Assessment

TRUST AND CULTURE EVALUATION TOOLS

In this section, we present a trust evaluation and a cultural assessment. The results of these day-long evaluations should provide an accurate representation of how trusting the organization is and the strength of its culture. These are tools for self-reflection, rather than empirical tools. They are meant to be subjective. The evaluation should encourage individuals to recognize trust in the organization.

Before proceeding with the assessment of trust, review the pillars of trust discussed in Chapter 4. The trust evaluation can be completed in one day. Whenever the evaluator observes a specific instance of trust, such as a demonstration of honesty or passion, during that day, he marks an *X* in box 1 in the appropriate row on the data collection sheet (Figure 9-9). If he sees another instance of honesty that day, he put an *X* in box 2 in that row.

At the end of the evaluation day, there should be a number of *X*s on the sheet. The pillar of trust marked most frequently is the strongest element of trust in the organization. Obviously, it would be ideal to end the day with a form completely filled with *X*s, but this is not very likely.

Trust Pillar	Demonstrations (or Observations) of Instances of Trust					
	1	2	3	4	5	6
Communication						
Predictability						
Honesty						
Credibility						
Passion						
Courage						
Competency						
Integrity						
Notes:						

Figure 9-9:   Instances of Trust

A very trusting organization should rate 4 or more—in other words, have four *X*s—in all categories. In this case, there is room for a little improvement, but more importantly, effort should be made to maintain the very trusting atmosphere. A trusting organization should rate 3 or more in all categories. It should look for ways to improve by noting the weakest elements of trust and working to understand the weaknesses.

If the organization rates less than 3 in all categories, then its leadership needs to determine why the organization is not a trusting one. Consider the other trust tools in this book to determine what types of problems the organization is having. If people are not acting as if they trust one another, then trust is not prevalent within the organization, which will cause many more problems.

To complete the cultural assessment, identify a group or person for observation. Over the course of a day, watch that group or person to see how many times the individuals demonstrate each of the eight attributes of organizational culture discussed in Chapter 6.

Whenever the evaluator observes behavior in accordance with any of the cultural attributes, she should mark an *X* in the first box in the correct row on the data sheet (Figure 9-10). If she sees another indication of that attribute, she should place an *X* in the second box in that row.

As for the trust evaluation, at the end of the evaluation day, a number of the boxes on the sheet will be marked. The row containing the most *X*s indicates the strongest cultural attribute in the organization. Again, it is not likely that the sheet will be completely full, although this is desirable.

Cultural Attributes	Demonstrations (or Observations) of Cultural Attributes					
	1	2	3	4	5	6
Innovation						
Risk Taking						
Attention to Detail						
Outcome Orientation						

People Orientation						
Team Orientation						
Aggressiveness						
Stability						
Notes:						

Figure 9-10: Cultural Assessment

In general, an organization with a very strong, positive culture should rate 4 or more in all categories. Some improvement is possible, but the organization should focus foremost on maintaining the strength of the culture. An organization that rates 3 or more in all categories has an effective culture, but its leadership should look at the attributes marked the fewest times, strive to understand why they appear to be weaker, and focus on improving them.

If the organization rates less than 3 in all categories, its leadership needs to determine why its culture is weak and make significant improvements. When people are part of an organization with a strong culture, they will seek to do the right thing. The culture determines, at least in part, what people do when they are not being monitored. When the eight cultural attributes discussed here are not prevalent within an organization, or if people do not connect to the organization's culture, they may act in a manner that is not congruent with whatever the culture is supposed to be—which can hurt the organization's reputation, among other possible problems. An organization without a strong culture tends to breed compliance issues and other problems. When other problems crop up in an organization with a weak culture, the real issue may be that the culture does not offer clear, positive guidelines for behavior in different circumstances.

This chapter offers evaluation tools that can be used when implementing or expanding a VPMO. They allow VPMO leaders to audit and monitor various aspects of the virtual organization, including its use of virtual elements, its culture, its ability to manage change, the level of trust in the organization, and more. The tools are designed to help direct VPMO leaders toward areas for improvement. They are useful in identifying problems or potential problems that could arise in a VPMO or during the implementation of a VPMO. The tools can be used as part of a continuous improvement process. They will not cost the organization a lot of money and are easy to use.

Remember that when using any tool, practice and consistency are important. Regularly using the tools will yield more accurate and reliable findings, indicating the norm for the VPMO. Establishing what is normal or typical for the organization is the first step toward determining how to improve it.

Chapter 10

LESSONS LEARNED AND BEST PRACTICES

Lessons learned are the shared knowledge that allows project managers and the organization to grow and projects to mature. A well-developed project management methodology has as a part of its closing process lessons learned. In fact, PMI's *PMBOK® Guide* (2008) states that lessons learned should be done as a part of the closing process group, processes that are done every time a management group ends. Beyond this, lessons learned should be collected throughout the life of a project.

Lessons learned are the lifeblood of a PMO—and this is even truer in a VPMO, though it is difficult to coordinate the collections of lessons learned and maintain them on a distributed/virtual project. Because in-person interactions are rare for virtual organizations (e.g., virtual teams don't have regular water cooler discussions), it becomes very important to facilitate the dissemination of lessons learned. If the mistakes made on one project aren't made known to future project team members, the virtual organization is more likely to make the same mistakes from project to project. The project manager should include lessons learned in the schedule within a schedule. All virtual aspects of the project must be followed within the main schedule, including the schedule within a schedule, for the virtual elements. Remember to create a separate WBS for virtual work items.

> **Best practice:** Always review lessons learned after a project is done. If done properly, this review will be painful for everyone involved, but it is worthwhile. There is always something to learn from a project, and there is always something that could have been done better.

BEST PRACTICES: AUTONOMY AND TRUST

Research has consistently shown that team autonomy, allowing teams to make decisions that affect themselves (Bourgault, Drouin, and Hamel 2008), and trust (Lipnack and Stamps 1997; Curlee and Gordon 2010; Curlee 2008; Webster and Wong 2008) are foundational to the success of virtual projects and, by extension, to the success of virtual organizations. Companies with leadership that drives and models these behaviors consistently get better results from their virtual projects. The VPMO needs to incorporate efforts that will encourage autonomy, decision-making, and trust into training, policies/procedures, best practices, and the schedule within a schedule for the virtual parts of a project.

For example, to build trust, project managers should be trained in providing guidance to team leads that will help the leads hold their team members accountable. Thus, not only must project managers hold project team leads accountable, they must ensure that team leads are holding their team members accountable. If the project manager and team leads fail to keep accountability alive on a project, the trust between team members and trust between subordinates and leaders and vice versa will deteriorate fast.

Normally, cliques are not desirable on projects; however, in the virtual environment, the project manager should encourage people to form their own teams. This will increase the level of trust on the project. When trust is mature on a virtual project and accountability and communication are working well, project teams will naturally form.

BEST PRACTICES FROM PMOS

Hobbs and Aubry (2008) found that the level of project management maturity in an organization helps to drive the decision-making authority of the PMO and hence its success. Extrapolating from this, PMOs that are involved in the organization's or company's strategic decision-making become entrenched in its daily activities and decision-making at the highest levels. The successful PMO no longer just reports status or audits projects.

A review of three case studies of successful PMOs—Lenovo, UK's Postcomm (the Postal Commission), and ESPN—revealed striking similarities, although the PMOs were established for very different reasons. Lenovo's PMO was purely administrative, intended to increase market share and improve business performance in China; Postcomm's was strategic and provided full support to leadership and projects; ESPN had a new CIO who needed a PMO to improve project maturity.

All three PMOs were linked into senior leadership and had senior leadership's complete support. Research shows that PMOs can survive for several years without senior leadership's sanction, but slowly the PMO will start to dwindle because middle management can no longer "conceal" the PMO within the organization (e.g., a skunkworks team) or find the dollars to continue the organization.

All three PMOs understood organizational culture, particularly ESPN's. The new CIO knew how important it was for the PMO to be one with the culture. What better way to connect the PMO and the company as a whole than with sports analogies? "Coaches" assisted the project manager, project portfolio and resource managers were called "league officials," sponsors were dubbed "umpires," and the PMO staff were called the "ground crew."

Lenovo understood that an administrative PMO that provided standardization and training and created links across the company to break down barriers would fit its culture. A PMO that assumed reporting, auditing, and strategic functions would have been rejected.

Culture was not addressed directly in the case study of Postcomm's PMO; however, some of the lessons learned were related to the organization's culture. For instance, pockets of the organization had a high level of project management maturity, but others did not. The lesson learned was that project sponsors should be assessed and level-setting should be done at the beginning of all projects. Also, the project managers expected to have a very tight relationship with the PMO. Whether this was due to the PMO leaders' own preferences or the nature of the organization is difficult to decipher from the case study.

Training and standardization were two other areas common to all three PMOs. While each one conducted different kinds of training, each PMO recognized what the organization or project managers needed, ensured it was funded, and provided the training. Lenovo's PMO had the most widespread effect on organizational standards. Leadership gave the PMO the authority to revamp corporate standards to include project management. This was not to bog down the training and standards process; rather, it was meant to enhance logistics and to understand where the process was at a given time.

All three PMOs were successful in their startup and ongoing operations. This success was driven by providing leadership support, understanding the culture of the organization, and delivering exactly what was expected. The leaders of the PMO understood that they had to satisfy two ends of the organizational spectrum: the strategic leadership and the project managers.

BEST PRACTICES FROM VIRTUAL ORGANIZATIONS

There is some research on virtual PMOs. Each of the VPMOs covered in the research we consulted for this book was a traditional PMO that was moved into a virtual setting. Best practices include:

- VPMOs do not always have to use the latest technology.
- A technological platform must drive the project management life cycle from end to end.
- The project approach should be disciplined and repeatable.
- "Virtualness" drives business value.
- Subject matter experts should be available throughout the company.

As would be expected, many of the best strategies focused on technology. When establishing policies and procedures for virtual projects, VPMO leaders must emphasize that technology must meet the needs of the project. Decisions about technology should not be driven by thoughts such as "We have to have the latest technology," or "We are using this technology because we have always used it." Technology must be evaluated for capability and compatibility with the infrastructure, especially if the project will be performed in a developing nation. The VPMO leadership needs to also assess its own technology for compatibility with the disbursed projects. If the VPMO itself is virtual, this adds another layer of complexity in establishing the VPMO and communicating with the virtual project managers. All this should be addressed when technology is discussed or if there are plans to change technology organization-wide.

Templates alone should not drive the project management life cycle. The project management methodology should be incorporated into a workflow package that allows for flexibility. Remember to allow feedback loops from the project manager, which will let her update the methodology and the workflow. Immediate changes may sometimes be necessary, depending on corporate policy and procedures and local laws in various countries.

In general, the VPMO must be able to justify its existence. The VPMOs in the research, which migrated to virtual environments from the normal PMO structure, were able to do so by decreasing overhead costs. The VPMO should provide value in several ways:

- It can save the organization money by being the center of "virtualness" for the company. In other words, the VPMO can drive the virtual portfolio and help senior leadership make the best decisions about virtual projects and programs.
- Resources can come in and out of virtual projects as needed, also potentially saving money.
- Project managers' skills sets will improve as they learn to lead virtual projects/programs.

It is obvious that virtual projects are *not* the same as traditional, collocated projects. This has been shown repeatedly in academic and industry research. Laws and culture in the United States and other countries affect the way individuals behave in managing their projects. Observing these laws and incorporating organizational and national culture into the VPMO's methodology, policies, standards, and procedures and providing training will reduce risk to the company and to project managers and team members. A VPMO must take into account that national culture is just as important as organizational culture. Preventing one lawsuit or fine can justify a VPMO's existence.

Best practice: What is the future of your VPMO? Does the organization have a plan to address continuity? Does the organization comply with Title IX of Public Law 110-53? Is there a plan to address a natural disaster or some other major disruption to the business? Virtual project management offices are susceptible to many technological disruptions, so such a plan is in the best interest of the organization.

Remember that virtual work has been performed since ancient times, as discussed in Chapter 2. What is different now is technology, particularly the existence of instant or near-instant communication. The common thread connecting all virtual organizations, regardless of their size or industry, is technology. In smaller companies or organizations, it is even more important to ensure that technology meets the requirements, rather than adapting the requirements to meet the technology. Smaller companies might lack the necessary funding to ensure that adequate technology is available. Too often, smaller companies try to operate as-is instead of investing in an effective IT infrastructure.

One company decided to use Google Apps for all of its employees' technological needs. The company had no brick-and-mortar spaces, and employees were located in the United States and Europe. Another company's two owners were located in Los Angeles, and both worked from their homes. They wanted to expand their market into New York City but did not want to travel or relocate there. Through technology and a virtual office space, the two owners were able to meet the needs of their New York City clients. Modern communications technology makes it possible for members of the same organization to live far apart. Not everyone has to coexist in the same area anymore. A virtual office equipped with proper technology (e.g., Internet access, email, social networking connections, webcam) is almost the same as occupying an office in the same building as others.

Large companies that have virtual organizations within their structure may not be as flexible as smaller ones in meeting virtual employees' technological needs. The IT infrastructure in large companies is normally set by the CIO's organization. It may be difficult for people in these companies to deviate from the tools chosen by the CIO, but it can be done. Virtual organizations within a larger company have written compelling business cases to support requests for technology that will meet a need for the smaller group.

Be aware of your organization's IT infrastructure, to understand its potential and its limitations. Deficiencies in the system should elicit a response from the organization to improve. If an organization stops improving, it might fall behind the competition.

Best practice: The competition is continually improving. Keep an eye on what others are doing, and make sure that your organization is not lagging behind.

Both traditional and virtual PMOs can use many of the same strategies to stay viable and successful. These include winning the support of senior leadership, understanding the culture of the organization and ensuring the PMO or VPMO mirrors those values, increasing project management maturity, and creating value for the leadership and project managers. In virtual organizations in particular, team autonomy, the freedom to make decisions that affect the VPMO, and trust are essential to success.

Technology best practices also are very important for virtual companies/organizations and VPMOs. It is not essential for companies to use the latest technology or own the technology. The driving factors behind the successful use of technology in the virtual environment are identifying all of the users' requirements and letting the requirements drive the technology. Technology should not be allowed to force compromises in the requirements.

PART IV

POLICIES, PROGRAMS, TRAINING, AND THE FUTURE

Beyond the topics already discussed, other matters are of concern to a VPMO, including laws, ethics, programs, and training. Figure IV-1 outlines the topics covered in the final chapters, 11–14.

Policies and Procedures, the Law, and Ethics
Policies and Procedures
The Sarbanes-Oxley Act
Working in Other Countries
Ethical Behavior

↓

Program Management
Strategic Planning
Aligning the Team around the Program Goal
Virtual Program Leadership

↓

Training
Determining What Kind of Training Is Necessary
Making the Right Kind of Training Available
Further Education

Looking Ahead
Why the PMO—and the VPMO—Are Here to Stay
The Future of the VPMO

Figure IV-1:   Additional Consideration for the VPMO

Chapter 11

POLICIES AND PROCEDURES, THE LAW, AND ETHICS

Policies, procedures, the law, and ethics are all important and interrelated concepts that a VPMO must address. VPMOs often operate in several different states or countries and possibly within different companies and entities, which means that they may be subject to—and trained in—various laws, policies, and procedures.

The most important thing to keep in mind is that compliance is not only a good idea, it is required. As the number of laws to which project organizations are subject continues to grow, it becomes even more essential for them to keep up with and understand those that affect them. Lawsuits seem to be becoming more prevalent, and some cash-strapped governments are diverting funds to auditing companies in order to generate revenue. Ignorance of the law is not a defense, and courts take a dim view of large multinational organizations that do not have an in-house expert to address all applicable laws.

> **Best practice:** Policy and procedure training is essential for any virtual project organization. How can you hold people accountable for following organizational policies and procedures if you do not periodically review them? Make sure to retrain even the experienced people to make sure they are aware of all policies and procedures.

POLICIES AND PROCEDURES

The virtual project management office is no different from any other organization. The VPMO must have solid and clear policies and procedures to guide all aspects of the organization. Policy and procedure manuals should not be the static documents they may have been in the past. Policies and procedures should be reviewed regularly to ensure that they are kept up-to-date.

The business world is changing quickly—for example, of the top 100 companies in the United States 50 years ago, very few are in existence today. Because of these changes, professions are transforming just as rapidly. People can no longer expect a stable profession as the number of relatively safe fields continues to diminish (Whymark and Ellis 1999). Every person employed today should expect to have a major change in the direction of their career every five to ten years.

Consider the following statistics on employment and organizational change. On average, businesses must replace 50 percent of employees in four years, 50 percent of their mid-level managers in five years, and 50 percent of their senior executives in seven years (King 1997). Obviously, organizational roles change quickly, so people should expect that their career, trade, or role will have a lifespan of no more than ten years. People who fail to adjust to new policies and procedures within their roles will find their skills outdated in several years.

> **Best practice:** Review your organization's ethics policy. Does it support the virtual project management office? Does it encompass all of the possible laws that relate to ethical behavior? Is there a social networking policy in place for the company? Does the policy exceed the minimum legal requirements, and by how much? Consider how the organization's ethics policy reflects the leadership of the virtual project management office. Consider what the policy says about leadership and how they are to behave.

One of the purposes of policies and procedures is to train a person for a particular role. The skills associated with that position might be important now, but they will mostly change within a few years. Policies and procedures should keep pace with these changes. So what can be done to keep policies and procedures up-to-date and people apprised of the changes, particularly in a VPMO? The only possible path is to make sure that there is a robust training program within the VPMO to continually update people on policies and procedures, and to ensure that there is a system for continually improving the existing policies and procedures.

Chapter 13 addresses training, so this section will review only how to implement continuous improvement with regard to policies and procedures. Continuous improvement is about the continual documentation of new and changing policies and procedures for a VPMO. There are two steps in this process. The first step is to appoint a custodian of policies and procedures, and the second step is to create accountability for the communication of new policies and procedures to the custodian.

Appointing a Custodian

Choosing a custodian is usually the easiest part of the process; appointing a person to a new task is generally not too difficult. Any problems usually arise later, if people do not communicate with the custodian on a timely basis.

The custodian will be responsible for compiling new policies and procedures and making sure these policies and procedures are shared with others. A good system for communicating policy and procedural changes is critical. Some believe (incorrectly) that virtual team members can be left alone, but in reality, virtual team members require clearer performance measures than collocated teams, and timely, continuous feedback is important. It keeps the project on track and keeps individuals focused on the goal(s) of the group (Duarte and Snyder 2006).

Ensuring Accountability

It is difficult to enforce a requirement that people report new policies and procedures in a timely manner. Some organizations put a time limit on submissions of new policies and procedures to create a sense of urgency, while others rely on informal channels for pre-implementation.

Regardless of the method, it is critical that the system be enforced. If people believe that the system can be ignored with no ill effects, then the system will be ignored. A good rule to follow is that if one does not see policy or procedure changes every month, then changes are going unreported or uncompleted. Inquire monthly to remind people of their responsibility to the VPMO to alert others—particularly the custodian—to these changes. Change is out there, but sometimes people do not realize that it is important enough to report, or they do not think that these changes matter to others.

Changes should come from all over the organization. Leaders and team members alike should offer new ideas to help improve any policy or procedure. Organizations that promote ideas from all levels will ultimately fare better than hierarchical organizations soliciting ideas only from management.

Best practice: Update the policy and procedure manual annually, at the very least. You will be surprised how many policies and procedures change in just one year. Making this a habit will not only keep the manual an active and living document, it will also make sure that people are aware of important changes.

THE SARBANES-OXLEY ACT

The Sarbanes-Oxley Act (SOX) is a set of laws enacted in 2002 that are designed to improve the information reliability of publicly traded corporations in the United States by increasing corporate responsibility for internal controls and external reporting. These laws, named after their sponsors in the Senate, came about in response to financial scandals at companies like WorldCom, Tyco, and Enron. *Corporate responsibility, policy,* and *compliance* are the key phrases associated with Sarbanes-Oxley.

Corporate Responsibility

At its core, SOX is about corporate responsibility. Be it signature authority, the reliability of information given to shareholders, fiscal controls, separation of duties, or organizational audits, SOX is intended to ensure that the information that leaves a company and that is presented to shareholders and others is accurate, true, and fair. In the past, there was little regulation of corporate information, and the requirements regarding the auditable nature of the information presented were weak. There will always be an element of risk inherent in participating in the stock market, but SOX's intent is to mitigate some of the blatant exaggerations that companies might make in the information they share.

Corporations are now more accountable for providing accurate, true, and fair information to the public. Corporate officers are also being personally held accountable for providing reasonable information on penalty of fines and even prison time. By holding corporate officials accountable, the government hopes to make sure that there are fewer public scandals caused by companies' dishonesty.

SOX also requires oversight of the public accounting firms responsible for auditing different corporations. One of the key factors in the wave of financial scandals that inspired SOX was that all of the firms involved had agreements with external auditing firms that should have been reporting any suspicious activities. Since there was no oversight, these audits were often not detailed enough, or the level of scrutiny was not close enough to find the problems. In some cases, problems were brought to the company's attention but were kept quiet. SOX requires that these accounting firms' findings be reviewed by the government (through the Public Company Accounting Oversight Board).

How do SOX's corporate responsibility requirements affect VPMOs? Everyone in the organization must understand that there is an individual and corporate responsibility to inform others when incorrect information (particularly of a financial nature) is reported. For example, individuals who know that an organization has underreported or overreported financials to shareholders are obligated to report the matter. They have a personal responsibility to contact the proper organizational authority and the government, if no other options are available, if the company purposely misleads the public. (This does not include honest mistakes.) It can be difficult to implement and enforce corporate responsibility measures in a virtual environment, where individuals are not always collocated and may not interact directly with one another.

Best practice: Send a copy of Sarbanes-Oxley to the entire team, and ask people to read it and verify receipt. Reading the law in full will prevent misunderstandings of the requirements.

Policy

A VPMO should have a SOX policy even if it is not a publicly traded company. The company should still attempt to adhere to the policies of SOX because responsible behavior helps maintain trust. An honest organization has nothing to fear from a SOX policy, but a deceptive one would have difficulty adhering to a SOX policy.

In general, a SOX policy must ensure that:

- Proper checks and balances exist within the organization, including signature limits and approvals.

- Proper care is taken to confirm information that is released about the company.

- Executives are responsible and accountable for the information being provided to the public. This responsibility is personal: fines and prison time can be levied against individuals, not just the corporation.

- Financial systems have controls to ensure that all spending is appropriately accounted for, regardless of where the money is spent within the organization.

- The policy regarding audits and financial systems is not subject to manipulation by other external or internal groups.

A typical policy should be sufficiently detailed to cover the SOX requirements, but it should also have some degree of flexibility to allow for slight changes in systems or processes. It must address authority and organizational approvals as well as govern external communication. Financial controls and audits need to be discussed and explained to all employees. This policy should be periodically updated, and organizations should pay attention to what other companies are doing to comply with this complex set of laws.

Organizations need to provide specialized SOX training. They should appoint a SOX expert and train her in the details of the law, the company SOX policy, best practices, and how the law impacts all aspects of the VPMO.

Best practice: Review your organization's policies pertaining to Sarbanes-Oxley and the FCPA. If the company lacks these policies or the rules are not covered or fully explained, contact the correct person in the organization to make sure that a policy is implemented. If the policy exists but is not particularly known or enforced, then the VPMO should make a project of ensuring that everyone is made aware of these important laws.

Compliance

SOX requires individual and corporate compliance. Corporate officers and management need to understand that there are individual and corporate requirements. Because this legislation is far-reaching and can affect many different elements of a VPMO, the organization should make sure that it has an appropriate policy that addresses these requirements. Compliance is about following procedures, and the VPMO has a much better chance of compliance if the policy is clear and is communicated to all affected individuals.

Corporate officers need to understand their responsibility to keep accurate financial records and to communicate correct and true information. Offering demonstrably incorrect or improper information will certainly raise the ire of auditors.

The VPMO must always be prepared for an audit. Again, the organization should appoint a SOX expert, who should conduct periodic SOX audits within the organization. It would not be unreasonable to conduct a SOX audit once a month to determine if the organization is in compliance. Internal audits are an excellent way to prepare everyone for a real SOX audit. The VPMO should not wait until external auditors are knocking on the door before finding out if the company SOX policy is in order. Increasing awareness of these regulations will help everyone make sure that compliance is a daily matter.

> **Best practice:** Review the organization's SOX policy annually to make sure that it is up-to-date and current. Procedures, roles, and divisions will change, so keeping this policy as accurate as possible is important, particularly if there is an audit. Not having an accurate Sarbanes-Oxley policy will surely capture the notice of an auditor.

WORKING IN OTHER COUNTRIES

One of the most common international management challenges is understanding which U.S. laws apply to U.S. citizens when they conduct business abroad. Almost all nations mandate that their citizens follow the laws of the country where the business is being done. So if one were to conduct business in the Philippines, one would expect to follow the laws of the Philippines. But U.S. citizens are expected to follow certain U.S. laws regardless of where they are working.

Business practices vary internationally, and some are very different from our own. For example, there is still considerable concern about bribery in foreign business. It is common practice in some countries to offer financial or other economic inducements to the government or business officials in order to cement a business relationship. Although other nations may allow such activities, in the United States, bribery is not only an ethical issue but a legal issue.

From a legal standpoint, bribery is described in the Foreign Corrupt Practices Act (FCPA) as the involvement of any U.S. citizen in a direct financial transaction above and beyond the norm for performing any business or governmental task. This law applies regardless of the laws where the incident took place. This law will supersede any other nation's law.

In brief, make sure that VPMO members understand that the law is the law and there are personal fines and penalties beyond the employment ramifications of breaking the law.

> **Best practice:** Consider a refresher regarding national and international laws whenever the virtual project management office is handling a multinational project. Laws can change so frequently that finding out the latest rules and regulations can only help the project. Prevention and education is always better than having an unfortunate incident during a project.

A VPMO will more than likely have some element of international activity, and the best way to handle international transactions is to either know the law exactly or to know exactly who the expert in this kind of law is. Since laws vary from nation to nation, and in most cases they are as intricate or as involved as the laws in the United States, it's important that VPMOs have a very clear understanding of the ones that affect their business. The laws governing purchasing are different from nation to nation, and these laws are completely different from the laws regarding income tax. Figure 11-1 illustrates the two-step process of addressing international law in a VPMO.

Step 1: Know the Transaction	>>	Step 2: Know the Expert

Figure 11-1: VPMO International Law Process

Know the Transaction

Step one is identifying the nature and type of the international transaction. Start by identifying whether the transaction is material or service related. If it is material-related, one should use the approved purchasing or procurement policy to handle the transaction. Although laws will vary internationally, perhaps the parties involved in the transaction can agree to follow the 1980 United Nations Convention on Contracts for the International Sale of Goods (CISG).

If the transaction is service-related, one must determine if it is a contracted or employment transaction. This decision will determine if the service provider will be maintained in a temporary or contract position or if he or they will become part of the organization on a permanent basis. The difference is important because it will help determine type of expert the organization chooses.

Know the Expert

Step two is determining the expert to engage. As discussed, if the transaction is for goods only, then it probably will only require using an approved purchasing process, and it can be governed under international standards such as the CISG. If the transaction is for temporary services, the organization might be able to use a purchasing process, but in this situation, it is wise to consult a lawyer or expert with experience in contracting in the nation in question. In some cases, one might be able to get the contracted party to agree to some standard terms and conditions, but it is a good idea to find out what the nation considers to be the governing law. Making sure that you are in compliance before you agree to a service contract is better than trying to explain your organization's actions in front of a foreign judge.

If the organization is attempting to hire people in another country, always consult legal counsel familiar with this process. Outsourcing, hiring of foreign nationals, and opening business in other nations is a complicated process in most cases, and it often leaves the contracting party open to many different types of liability. FCPA holds U.S. firms responsible for the vendors and subcontractors they hire, even though they may be local nationals.

In conclusion, knowing the transaction and knowing the experts are both essential. There are too many variables to address here; we will simply say that a VPMO will likely become involved in international transactions, so understanding the process for doing so is the best way to start. Knowing who to ask in advance is better than having to find a good lawyer to get out of an unfavorable situation.

ETHICAL BEHAVIOR

Laws such as the Foreign Corrupt Practices Act may address the financial implications of business transactions, but the ethical implications of offering non-financial consideration is an area of additional concern and is not clearly addressed in law. Ethically speaking, individuals must not offer any undue consideration to individuals by offering or accepting any preferential treatment. In order to control this type of behavior, many international organizations have ethical standards that are not just a matter of written policy, but require individuals to sign legally binding documents agreeing to behave ethically in such circumstances. Such a policy might read:

> [The company's] intent is to adhere to a strict policy of fair competition. Suppliers are not to pay any sum of money or give anything of value whatever, directly or indirectly, in order to lessen or destroy free competition.

A policy like this would help ensure that the ethical choice would be made in an ambiguous situation. Managers who deal globally must understand that even some ethical rules that seem obvious may not apply in other nations.

A manager must be aware of potential conflicts that may arise and must remain informed when doing business internationally. When working internationally, either in person or virtually, managers should take nothing for granted. Keep in mind that managers' title or presence may lend greater credibility or visibility to whatever they do or do not do. Remember that others are watching; culturally inappropriate behavior only serves to further justify the belief of some that managers from the United States are less educated and less aware than their overseas counterparts.

For example, in the United States, you might not consider it an ethical issue to communicate with people from other companies. In fact, many managers learn more from speaking directly to counterparts at other companies than perhaps by any other means. This kind of social networking helps keep individuals in touch with the industry. In other nations, such as Japan, it would be a huge ethical issue to speak to individuals in a competing company. Business relationships trump social relationships, and it is common to sever ties with individuals that end up working for the competition.

Any virtual organization or project must have a set of ethical requirements for everyone involved, including subcontractors or other consultants. Organizations should not allow any leeway for intermediaries to handle matters unethically—seemingly under the direction of the organization. Make sure to have all parties involved in the organization or project sign an ethics agreement, verifying that they understand the ethical requirements of the organization.

Keep in mind that what is considered culturally acceptable or ethical behavior may shift from project to project, depending on the circumstances. For example, in the United States, it is not uncommon to apply an interest rate to unpaid or late invoices. However, in Islamic nations, money lending is illegal, so one must be careful when working with people in those countries. A call from a pushy accounts receivable person demanding an interest payment might make for an awkward, culturally insensitive situation.

You might find yourself in an ethical quandary when employees in a certain country are less stringent about deadlines. Or you might yourself challenged by individuals who do not adhere to deadlines and appear to always take a less-serious view of the implications. Certain nations have a different sense of urgency about deadlines, and, as a result, it could be difficult to ask certain international team members to respect deadlines.

Best practice: At the beginning of any new virtual project, consider what kinds of updates to the ethics policy might be necessary to align organizational ethical behavior with the project. Understanding international ramifications, if applicable, can help the VPMO avoid any unpleasant situations during the project.

The axiom "Measure twice and cut once" is just as applicable to the law as it is to carpentry. In other words, being prepared is key. Researching applicable laws in advance is much better than finding out what the laws are after one is already in trouble; keep in mind that ignorance is not an excuse. VPMOs may have to comply with the Sarbanes-Oxley Act; even if they do not, it is advisable for them to have a policy aligned with the provisions of the act. Most VPMOs will engage in international work, so awareness of other countries' laws as well as U.S. laws that apply to citizens working outside the country is essential. International law experts can help ensure compliance.

Ethical behavior is also important, and VPMOs should consider developing written ethics policies. Policies and procedures in general must be kept up-to-date, and policy and procedure training is essential.

Chapter 12

PROGRAM MANAGEMENT

The *PMBOK® Guide* defines *program management* as "the centralized coordinated management of a program to achieve the program's strategic objectives and benefits" (Project Management Institute 2008, p. 10). It defines a program as "a group of related projects managed in a coordinated way to obtain benefits and control not available from managing them individually. Programs may include elements of related work outside of the discrete projects in the program" (Project Management Institute 2008, p. 9). A very large project may in some cases be called a program, but here we use the PMI definition of the term to ensure a common understanding.

Seasoned project managers often manage multiple projects at a time, and one or several of those may be virtual. What a company's management may not understand is that distributed projects present certain complexities that do not exist in traditional projects. The VPMO should act as the virtual project manager's advocate by reviewing the number of projects assigned to various project managers, evaluating their complexity, and demonstrating that virtual projects are by nature complex. This will particularly help project managers who are managing many distributed projects. The VPMO should track resource requirements and forecasts. By monitoring resources and the bandwidth of each individual in a project management function, the VPMO can provide adequate staffing for projects with minimal bench time. Also, the VPMO should assess virtual project managers' performance in leading virtual projects. Those whose work is marginal to failing should be given targeted training, tips, and tools for leading virtual projects.

STRATEGIC PLANNING

The VPMO can help with the organization's strategic planning by reviewing all of the organization's virtual projects, traditional projects, and ongoing operations to see if it can uncover any hidden programs.

It may have to work with another PMO in doing so and in supporting virtual parts of a program. It is recommended that one project management office take the lead in supporting a given program.

As noted, programs are established to provide control and increase benefits to projects. Imagine that the CEO of a company has stated that the company needs to increase sales by 15 percent over the next three years. The organization has 15 independent projects, some virtual, some traditional, related to this goal of increasing sales by 15 percent. For example, some projects include new sales tools, but does it make sense for the company to have multiple sales tools? A better approach would be to have the VPMO assess the 15 independent projects. Determine if the projects can realistically meet the strategic objective of increasing sales by 15 percent over the next three years. If the VPMO leader determines that by grouping these projects together the organization would benefit more by controlling the effort altogether, rather than managing individual projects, then it should be done (Project Management Institute 2008).

Program managers develop processes and procedures to direct and control projects that are interrelated. At the beginning of a program, they must develop a benefits realization plan, the objectives of which the program must meet. A benefits realization plan outlines the benefits the program will deliver to the company or organization over the life of the program and program deliverables. It shows how implementing each project in the program will achieve the goal of the program. Normally, a program's strategic objectives have not been met by the end of a program. A benefits realization plan includes certain targets that are measured after the program is dissolved. This is to ensure the program has lasting value to the organization.

The benefits realization plan is a living document. It will change over the life of a program. Technology, stakeholders' wants and needs, and the market may change over a program's duration. The program manager may have to accelerate some projects to the detriment of other projects. This may be catastrophic for the individual project manager, but it should not be for the program. The VPMO needs to provide appropriate training to project managers so that they will understand these dynamics.

ALIGNING THE TEAM WITH THE PROGRAM GOAL

The program manager or project manager of multiple projects has to make the end goal of the program or each project clear. The way to do this is to communicate, communicate, then communicate some more. Once a project is in the execution phase and everyone is busy and facing challenges, the last thing anyone wants to hear is talk about the program or project goals, but it is the program manager's responsibility to talk about them. As emphasized earlier in this book, communication is especially difficult in the distributed environment. The program manager and project managers within the program can work in tandem to make it easier. The program manager should ensure that the project managers understand the program goal and have communicated it to their project personnel.

The astute virtual program manager mandates formal audits and informal reviews as a part of the schedule of each component project. As each audit or review is completed, positive results should be celebrated, or missteps should be used as lessons learned. At no time should a discussion of lessons learned be used as a "gotcha" session for the project/program team. Use this session to reemphasize the program's final goal, emphasize what was done well, and provide training or coaching on any weaknesses on the project. Constantly remind everyone about the importance of responsibility, accountability, and communication.

In addition to audits, reviews, and meetings, the program manager should also establish other forms of communication. She can:

- Start a program newsletter—what better way to remind people of the program goal than in print?
- Work to showcase the program in a company newsletter.
- Set her email tagline to be the program goal.
- Occasionally ask what the program goal is during internal meetings.

By rallying the team around one common theme and making sure team members understand its importance, it is easier to get everyone facing the same way.

VIRTUAL PROGRAM LEADERSHIP

Many have said that brute force is necessary to complete a program. This may be true of a traditional program, but this approach will not work in a virtual program. Transformational leadership is one of the best styles to use in the virtual environment. Transformational leaders set high performance criteria for their subordinates and model correct behavior for the team.

Virtual projects and especially virtual programs work on the edge of complexity. The program manager hardly ever sees or never sees the program team and may not even communicate with some of its members; some team members work on areas that may be invisible to the program manager, except through the schedule and status reports; and at any given time, the program could be on the brink of chaos. Complexity theory, as applied to projects and programs, argues that projects and programs are not linear (Curlee and Gordon 2010).

Complexity theory makes nonlinear organizations—organizations that do not operate from a traditional hierarchical structure—possible. A colony of ants operates the same way. The worker ants operate independently without asking permission from the queen ant before taking action to benefit the colony. The queen never sees or communicates with the vast majority of colony members, but when disaster strikes, each insect knows what it must do and does it. Each also knows what to do under normal circumstances, as should virtual program or project team members. Virtual programs or projects should function similarly.

A virtual program or project manager needs to have sufficient experience in the virtual environment to successfully lead a virtual endeavor. If the leader has experience, he or she can direct the team towards the goal. Note that although program managers should ideally have some prior experience working on a virtual team, a lack of virtual experience is rarely a reason for failure on a virtual project (Duarte and Snyder 2006).

The virtual program manager should measure individual and team performance. This will help to reduce conflict and underscore the manager's expectations of high performance. Team members will want to recognize progress as well, and they will want to understand how everyone is contributing. If certain team members' contributions aren't recognizable, others will feel that those team members are not pulling their weight. If the program team does not see how it's faring in its efforts to reach its goals, members can lose focus or feel demoralized.

Evaluating performance should also help mitigate the effects of a lack of face-to-face communication on the project and keep the team focused on short- and long-term goals (Curlee and Gordon 2010). Individuals who receive feedback on their performance will be better equipped to deal with any deficiencies. Most people want to overlook their weaknesses; having constructive conversations about a team member's weaknesses will help him or her face and respond to the information. The VPMO can help the program manager establish appropriate metrics, which can assist in showing the team how the program is progressing.

Best practice: Always set top goals. Asking people to try harder is important for success—and succeeding at a difficult task creates a feeling of real achievement.

Transformational leaders provide feedback to individuals and teams. The performance metrics the program manager uses and his high expectations may make him seem like a taskmaster. To justify his expectations, the program manager must always be able to explain how the metrics he uses are tied to milestones to achieve success. The program manager must make clear that he is an advocate for the team by providing the tools its members need. The program manager should provide systems, technology, communication, and any other specialized equipment necessary to complete the needed tasks and to stay in touch with others on the team. Here again, the VPMO can help the program manager by making sure the program team has the technology necessary to run an efficient program.

The VPMO may be focused initially on projects, but there is nothing that prevents it from also providing support and leadership to virtual programs. VPMO staff should understand that programs are strategic in nature, so a program will probably combine traditional projects and virtual projects. If the VPMO has to collaborate with another PMO and there has not been any previous collaboration, tension may arise. For the program's sake, only one PMO can take the lead.

When VPMOs decide to support programs, their staff must understand that a program is not just a big project—it is a collection of projects that provide a clear strategic objective to the company or organization. The VPMO should understand the company's strategic goals, which it can learn more about by reviewing all of the company's projects and programs, virtual and traditional.

Virtual program managers have a complex and essential role that includes developing a program benefits realization plan, auditing and reviewing projects, communicating with program team members, evaluating individual and team performance, and giving feedback.

Chapter 13

TRAINING

The traditional PMO and the VPMO may overlap in the types of training they offer, if they offer training, which not all PMOs do. Some partner with the company's training organization to design the training or provide subject matter expertise for project management courses. PMO leaders should be advocates for project management training, especially in companies in which project management maturity is low. Training leadership on the merits of project management and demonstrating the advantages of the PMO or the VPMO can be what the leaders need to become project management advocates!

DETERMINING WHAT KIND OF TRAINING IS NECESSARY

PMOs should provide targeted training to various groups depending on their needs. The leadership within the PMO must stay current in the discipline of project management and business practices. Project management encompasses the bigger picture of portfolio management, program management, project management, and any other areas as defined by the Project Management Institute.

Projects are affected by business and in turn affect business, and the PMO staff needs to understand this relationship. For example, when the Sarbanes-Oxley Act became law, many companies struggled to figure out how implement its requirements in a cost-effective and transparent manner. Astute project management leaders realized that project management was a viable, cost-effective option for complying with the act. Those companies that had trained their project managers in business theory as well as project management reaped the rewards of forward thinking and using project management in a nontraditional role.

In a virtual project management office, training and learning are major factors in the virtual environment's success (Townsend and DeMarie 1998; Duarte and Snyder 2006). Specifically, training in communication and communication technology is imperative because the virtual project management office is dependent on technology (Townsend and DeMarie 1998). Learning is about making sure that the organization has the right resources, policies, and procedures in place to support the organization.

Three important factors should be present in any kind of training program a VPMO develops or uses:

- The training program must train for the technology available and should include virtual tools.
- The VPMO must promote learning as an organizational value.
- The VPMO needs to teach some level of competency and appreciation for project management and project management skills.

Training in Technology

Townsend and DeMarie's (1998) studies indicate that technology training should occur more often for virtual organizations than for traditional teams since technology is the mainstay for communication in the virtual environment and is evolving at a fast pace.

To determine what training in technology is necessary, there must be an initial assessment of the existing technology and level of competence. An initial assessment will help determine what kind of technology is currently deployed, while addressing any potential training issues. Equity of technology and training and consistency in training yield benefits for the VPMO and its projects. When all team members are treated equitably, everyone feels valued. If one group is offered training and another is not, one group will be privileged and the other will be considered less desirable. If everyone is given the same training, the organization will be building a team on which everyone will want to work together. A VPMO that has tiers of individuals because of differences in available technology or training will likely be inefficient, because some groups will have difficulty working with other groups due to a feeling of inequality or worse.

Use a technology training evaluation form like the one shown in Figure 13-1 to gather important information about all project stakeholders' level of comfort with each recommended project system. This information can be used to determine whether individual or small-group training to improve stakeholders' skill level with the project systems would be most appropriate.

Stakeholder's Name:	Division/Project:	
NAME OF SYSTEM and VERSION NUMBER	LEVEL OF PROFICIENCY	NECESSARY TRAINING
	High - Medium - Low	Entry - Basic - Advanced
	High - Medium - Low	Entry - Basic - Advanced
	High - Medium - Low	Entry - Basic - Advanced

Figure 13-1: Technology Training Evaluation

Promoting Learning

A virtual project management office must also promote learning. People are more likely to learn when someone who is considered a subject matter expert and is trusted teaches them. It is also important to deliver the training experience in a credible environment and to facilitate a credible experience. A credible training environment and experience is a stimulating, interesting place that builds skills that participants themselves are eager to learn. Don't impose training as a prison sentence.

Ad hoc training might work well for certain individuals, but additional training is needed to promote real learning. Learning should be integrated into the culture of the VPMO. An organization's culture drives its values. If people with training and experience are valued, then others will want to become like them. If, on the other hand, experience is considered a liability, this mentality must be changed quickly, or most training will not be successful. To do this, reward and acknowledge real training in a way that highlights the real value of the training. Rewarding training personnel, for example, will show how the organization values training. If the organization makes it seem as though training is an expense to be avoided, then people will not be eager for or feel comfortable pursuing training. Organizations should value training and show how it improves satisfaction.

Training in Project Management

The training program must include some level of training in project management, or training should connect back to project management. Since a PMO or a VPMO is fundamentally a project-driven organization, the training provided needs to reflect those roots.

Regardless of whether the organization trains a wide spectrum of people as project managers or creates project-management specialist teams to handle projects, the organization must train people in applying project management skills to their tasks. Even an employee working in the accounting department, the logistics department, or the training department would benefit from project management training. These employees may need only a limited amount of training in project management (accountants are not often called upon to head software development projects), but it benefits the organization if everyone understands the goals, needs, and requirements of a project manager. All tasks can become projects, and so by applying project and time management skills to all tasks, an organization can become substantially more effective and efficient. The more effective and efficient an organization is at the lowest level, the greater its efficiency and competitive advantage will be.

Even if the training is review, more training always yields benefits. Professional athletes train and train and train on the basics of their trade. A quarterback will practice passing the ball, and a soccer player will practice kicking the ball—and each and every time they practice, they learn something new. Such practice might seem like routine, but the athletes know that every throw or kick is different, and during a game, every one counts. Organizational training is exactly the same thing. There are no chances to start a situation over from the beginning to do it better the second time. Every project decision counts, and one wrong decision might doom a project. Training prepares people to make good decisions.

Training is a continuous process, not an end to a means. Constant training helps ensure the survival of an organization. Without training, project management skills (like most skills) become dated and less effective. If a PMO or VPMO were to stop training, the skill level of its people would decline, and the organization would slowly lose focus. Thus, PMOs and VPMOs need to make the most of training and ensure that it is continually available, and organizations must actively promote learning as a core value.

MAKING THE RIGHT KIND OF TRAINING AVAILABLE

Training needs for a VPMO should be structured to meet the needs of the project managers in the field and to increase organizational project maturity. Since virtual project managers are remote, the VPMO staff needs to make training accessible, which means that most training will be Internet-based. The VPMO should also evaluate the types of training it offers, if applicable (not all VPMOs offer training, but they should be advocates of project management training). This evaluation will help ensure that appropriate training is being offered. No team is static, so as team members join the organization, make sure everyone is properly trained. Too often, organizations offer training once a year and feel like that's enough to get the job done. Training isn't done until everyone is properly trained and kept up-to-date with changing technology and information.

The VPMO staff must work with the organization's legal department to design training on laws that affect projects in the United States and internationally. The legal department should advise the VPMO on how laws in various countries affect U.S. corporations and what employees of those corporations must do to comply with those laws. For instance, the Foreign Corrupt Practices Act allows for paying a government official in a foreign country to expedite packages through customs, but it does not allow bribery. Legal advice can help clarify exactly what is allowed and what constitutes a bribe. Legal training should also be responsive to current events: laws normally do not change drastically overnight, but in some countries, political instability could change the way projects must be done.

In addition to training in project management and applicable laws, virtual project managers need training in culture, particularly when working on a cross-cultural project. The VPMO and human resources department can work together to coordinate cultural training (visit http://www.state.gov/m/fsi/tc/79756.htm for culture-training resources). Cultural training increases awareness even if the project is performed entirely in the United States. Team members' cultural backgrounds may not be as visible on a domestic project, unless the team holds conference calls and regional accents can be heard. Some people still make assumptions about others based on where they come from: Southerners are thought to be slow and lazy, while Northerners are characterized as cold-natured and rude, and folks from California are said to be laid-back. Training helps people discard stereotypes, break down any cultural barriers, and learn how to work with and respect people from other cultures.

The VPMO needs to train everyone working on virtual projects in the differences between virtual and traditional work. Topics that should be covered include how to monitor trust and hold individuals accountable in a virtual environment; how to interview potential team members and assess them for compatibility with a virtual environment; how to deal with conflict on a virtual project; and keeping a schedule within the schedule for the virtual elements of a project.

Sponsors need training as well. A sponsor must understand the difficulties the virtual project manager faces in the field, how virtual projects differ from traditional ones, and how the sponsor's own role will differ from what it would be on a traditional project. The VPMO should provide same kind of training to other stakeholders in the project management organization.

FURTHER EDUCATION

People working in project management can enhance their knowledge and differentiate themselves by earning a new degree or a relevant certificate. This is one way to show that one is serious about learning more and is committed to the field; completing a long-term program, not just a short-term management development course, shows a serious level of commitment.

> **Best practice:** Consider completing a project management degree or certificate through an institution like DeVry's Keller Graduate School of Management, Northcentral University, or Boston University.

Part of the VPMO's role as the advocate for project management is coordinating training. Whether the VPMO is directly or indirectly responsible for training or does not focus on training, its staff must ensure that people working on virtual projects get the necessary training in project management, culture, legal and ethical issues, finance, business, and other topics as applicable. The VPMO needs to stay in tune with the company, industry, and project management to understand what should constitute training for project managers, teams, sponsors, and other stakeholders. Individuals also can take the initiative and pursue more education related to project management.

Chapter 14

LOOKING AHEAD

As companies' competitors continue to reduce costs and improve efficiency, creating a VPMO to support virtual work has never been more pressing. Some organizations may continue to resist the idea of creating a VMPO, but organizational leadership needs to consider some of the core benefits:

- The VPMO will continually assess virtual project management throughout the organization, which will improve the likelihood of project success.

- The VPMO standardizes project management best practices throughout the entire virtual organization. This will allow project teams all over the world to benefit from the experience of their counterparts. It should also improve the use and communication of best practices.

- The VPMO should improve communication; everyone from senior executives to stakeholders will get important updates about every organizational project.

- The VPMO should improve decision-making, which will help projects achieve their strategic objectives.

- The VPMO improves processes and has other economically beneficial effects, so it should not be perceived as a cost center.

With these benefits in mind, every organization that does virtual work can and should create a VPMO, expand its use of VPMO techniques, or shift an existing PMO to a full-fledged VPMO. The sooner organizations start to think about how a VPMO can help their virtual projects, the sooner they will achieve project success.

WHY THE PMO—AND THE VPMO—ARE HERE TO STAY

The PMO is here to stay because, simply put, it offers so many benefits to organizations. The *PMBOK® Guide* lists many different reasons for an organization to adopt a PMO. The same reasons apply to VPMOs. The benefits of a PMO and a VPMO include:

- Shared resources across all projects administered by the PMO
- Coordinated resources across the organization
- Improvements in project methodology, including best practices and standards
- A shared repository for information regarding risk, project policies, procedures, templates, tools, and project documentation
- A unified and consistent configuration for all projects administered by the PMO
- Centralized communication management across projects
- Coordination of project standards
- Mentoring and development programs for project managers
- Enterprise-level monitoring of project timelines and budgets.

THE FUTURE OF THE VPMO

The future of the VPMO is growth. There is no doubt that more organizations will implement VPMOs. The VPMO offers a clear and proven strategy for success. By becoming more virtual, an organization can reap greater financial rewards, create value for its stakeholders, and even help the planet by reducing projects' environmental impact.

Some might still ask, if an organization already has a successful PMO, why should it change? If a PMO is already capturing project business, why force employees to go virtual, and why create a whole new entity? The reason for creating a VPMO is, quite simply, economics. Ultimately, PMOs are more likely to succeed with more opportunities than with fewer. A VPMO has more opportunities than a PMO, and more opportunities equate to more financial success.

A VPMO, particularly a multinational one, can successfully deploy project teams to different locations in order to complete important projects for which collocation is not really a requirement. Consider for a moment whether collocation is truly necessary when a company is developing a new software package. A traditional

PMO would probably want to deploy the project team with the programmers in order to keep everyone together. Approaching the work this way can certainly be successful, but consider the expense. Is deploying everyone the right financial decision?

An established VPMO allows a project team to interact, operate, and complete the project without having to be in close physical proximity. Related to this, a VPMO is able to offer a much more competitive price than a PMO because it can control costs and keep overhead down, as it does not have to support a large business office and infrastructure. The decreased costs of capital and overhead will certainly allow the VPMO to offer more competitive proposals. A VPMO, then, has a serious economic advantage over a PMO, not only because it saves the VPMO money on the cost of projects but because it helps the organization win more project business. On top of the cost advantages, a VPMO can offer a wider selection of skilled professionals, possibly from all over the world, to work on a given project.

We can see that the benefits of delving into virtual work and building a VPMO clearly outweigh the costs, but organizations' management teams must have the resolve to make the change. Organizations must stop watching history passing them by. They must commit to becoming a part of history by joining the VPMO movement.

Glossary

Aggressiveness—A cultural attribute that has often been discounted because the word has negative connotations. However, positive aggressiveness is what drives risk taking and innovation.

Attention to detail—A cultural attribute. In project management, the devil is in the details. In organizations that focus on attention to detail, top quality is always important, and even minor details are handled as a project crisis.

Change breaker—A person who resists change. There are different kinds of change breakers; some resist change directly and overtly, some indirectly and covertly. No matter their method, change breakers are obstacles to change.

Change maker—Usually a leader in the organization. He is a driven individual who wants to change some aspect of the organization—but he may not have changes *other* people want to make on his agenda, especially if those changes will affect him.

Change taker—Someone who has considered the negatives and positives of a change and has concluded that the change is good. Once a change taker is convinced that the change is positive, he will accept it and move on. Most people resist change initially because they fear or dislike the unknown, so it's unusual for someone to be a change taker from the outset. People are more likely to act as change takers once they understand how a change will benefit them.

Communication—The first pillar of trust. Research has shown that the most robust form of communication—and the one that is most likely to build trust—is one-on-one personal interaction in which the parties consider themselves equals, despite their position in the organizational hierarchy.

Competency—One of the eight pillars of trust that means having sufficient skill or knowledge to do what is necessary. A leader must be competent in her role, and she should have a high degree of expertise in a particular area of the project. She does not need to excel or even be competent in every role on a project, but she must understand the work to be done on a high level.

Contingency—One of the four organizational change management strategies discussed in this book. It involves planning and preparing for the unexpected, which is the mantra of the successful project manager.

The project manager should consider what might happen if a change fails, is delayed, or is resisted.

Courage—One of the eight pillars of trust that means a willingness to stand up for one's beliefs, challenge others, and admit mistakes. Project managers must demonstrate courage, as this kind of behavior will build trust in the project manager and in any project she is a part of.

Credibility—One of the eight pillars of trust that means the ability of a leader to influence his constituency based on his personal values and reputation. A credible leader does what he says he will do. Credibility is also about doing the right thing at the right time based on what one believes.

Delegation—Passing responsibility to another person. Project managers can delegate some of their duties to team members. For example, when a project is being planned, the virtual project manager should consider appointing a project historian to handle some of the project communication tasks.

Foreign Corrupt Practices Act (FCPA)—To reduce corruption and the bribery of foreign officials, congress enacted the FCPA in 1998 in an attempt to eliminate U.S.-related corruption and money laundering. The FCPA is also supported by 33 other countries to decrease corruption by high government and military officials. It had been observed that private industry had been targeting foreign nations in an attempt to exploit financial gain or commercial advantage. Since this legislation is directed at U.S. citizens operating abroad, rather than to enforce just the law of the impacted nation, it will have a profound and long-term impact on how business is conducted by U.S. citizens in the international marketplace (World-Check 2011).

Honesty—One of the eight pillars of trust that means telling the whole truth. Project managers need to pass along all of the information that is available. Telling half-truths makes a person appear dishonest.

Human interaction (HI)—The element of communication that includes asking questions and answering them and solving problems. Interaction helps reinforce the message being presented. In a traditional organization, where all parties are available for an impromptu discussion or clarification, this can happen in person. HI needs to be enabled by technology on a virtual project.

Innovation and risk taking—An attribute of organizational culture. A culture that actively supports innovation and risk taking is one that encourages finding solutions to problems, even when the problems are not impeding the current project.

Integrity—One of the eight pillars of trust. A project manager with integrity respects himself, the team, and others; more specifically, he respects others' beliefs and the personal culture of individuals and the team. He makes an effort to do the right thing for the team.

Outcome orientation—A cultural attribute. Project-based companies are driven by outcome—in other words, they are outcome-oriented. The ultimate goal is the successful launch of a project. A project-based company demands results beyond established expectations.

Passion—One of the eight pillars of trust. A leader must display passion for the task and passion for the project. Beyond the project, a successful project manager must also express an interest in the team, the organization, and the community. Making a convincing argument for a cause you believe in is an expression of passion.

People orientation—A cultural attribute. It is the recognition that people make the culture; the culture does not make the people, and that people are what make projects successful. A people-oriented culture supports individuals in the organization.

Planning the path—One of the four organizational change management strategies discussed in this book. Successful projects are never delivered on time and on budget by accident—there is always a good reason. Whenever a change is expected, a good project manager should spend considerable time planning in advance to organize every dimension of a projected change. All change projects must have a beginning, a middle, and an end.

Political follower—Someone who makes sure that her projects fulfill the objectives of the organization.

Political leader—Someone who advertises her projects, which is important in a virtual environment because project teams might not be able to have water cooler chats with others in the organization. Leaders who talk up their work will "sell" more—attract more interest—than those that do not seek out "customers."

Political victim—Project managers who do not bother to advertise their projects, then learn that the projects are not fully supported by the organization, become political victims. If a project is not integrated into the organization, the project manager might find himself out of a project—and even out of a job.

Predictability—One of the eight pillars of trust that is important because it allows team members to understand the project manager's expectations and the needs of the project. People will follow a predictable project manager—usually because they understand her expectations.

Project—A temporary endeavor undertaken to create a unique product, service, or result (Project Management Institute 2008, p. 5).

Project manager—The person assigned by the performing organization to achieve the project objectives (Project Management Institute 2008, p. 13).

Relegation—Delaying responding to stakeholders for the sake of saving time and ensuring clarity in communication. It is a way to compartmentalize requests for information and to more efficiently communicate information and expectations about the information.

Responsibility—One of the four organizational change management strategies discussed in this book. Understanding who is responsible is necessary if change is to actually happen. If no one is responsible for a change, nothing gets done because there is no incentive to achieve the desired results.

Sarbanes-Oxley (SOX) Act—A set of laws enacted in 2002 that are designed to improve the information reliability of publicly traded corporations in the United States by increasing corporate responsibility for internal controls and external reporting. These laws, named after their sponsors in the Senate, came about in response to financial scandals at companies like WorldCom, Tyco, and Enron. *Corporate responsibility*, *policy*, and *compliance* are the key phrases associated with Sarbanes-Oxley.

Speed—One of the four organizational change management strategies discussed in this book. Speedy change benefits the organization. Dragging out change can be painful and damaging. Changes fail because projects are frozen by politics or committees more often than for any other reason.

Team orientation—An attribute of organizational culture. Teams are very important in a virtual organization's culture. The more that people feel that they are part of a team, the better off the organization will be because the feeling of being included will generate loyalty and trust.

Virtual—The manner in which non-collocated people in an organization or on a team work together. They rely on technology to collaborate, conduct business, and share ideas. Face-to-face meetings are not a necessity (Majchrzak et al. 2004), nor are they always possible.

Virtual project—Sometimes referred to as a *disbursed project*, more than 50 percent of the project team members are not resident in the same physical location, though they are not necessarily dispersed over different time zones. Team members depend on technology to communicate, rarely or never meet face-to-face more than once every two weeks, and are allowed to make decisions about the project (Kelley 2001; Townsend and DeMarie 1998; Maznevski and Chudoba 2000).

Visuals and voice (V&V)—The primary vehicle of information transfer. Visuals can include written words, displays, and charts, as well as videos. Recordings or live verbal communication are examples of voice.

References

Anderson, E., D. Doyle, P. Friedlander, D. Schroeder, and T. Seymour. 1998. Telecommuting Primer. *Infotech Update* 7: 1.

Bass, B., ed. 1990. *Bass & Stogdill's handbook of leadership: Theory, research, and managerial applications.* 3rd ed. New York: The Free Press.

Bolman, L. G., and T. E. Deal. 2003. *Reframing organizations: Artistry, choice, and leadership.* San Francisco: Jossey-Bass.

Boudreau, M., K. Loch, D. Robey, and D. Straud. 1998. Going global: Using information technology to advance the competitiveness of the virtual transnational organization. *Academy of Management Executive* 12 (November): 120–128.

Bourgault, M., N. Drouin, and E. Hamel. 2008. Decision making within distributed project teams: An exploration of formalization and autonomy as determinants of success. *Project Management Journal* 39 (August): S97–S110.

Cascio, W. 2000. Managing a virtual workplace. *Academy of Management Executive* 14 (August): 81–90.

Curlee, W. 2008. Modern virtual project management: The effects of a centralized and decentralized project management office. *Project Management Journal* 39 (August): S83–S96.

Curlee, W., and R. Gordon. 2010. *Complexity theory and project management.* Hoboken, NJ: John Wiley & Sons, Inc.

Duarte, D., and N. Snyder. 2006. *Mastering virtual teams.* 3rd ed. San Francisco: Jossey-Bass.

Eigen, L. D., and J. P. Siegel. 1989. *The manager's book of quotations.* Rockville, MD: AMACOM.

Elkins, T. 2000. Virtual teams. *IIE Solutions* 32 (April): 26–31.

Furst, S. A., M. Reeves, B. Rosen, and R. S. Blackburn. Managing the life cycle of virtual teams. *Academy of Management Executive* 18 (May): 6–20.

Garrett, G. A. 2007. *World class contracting*. 4th ed. Riverwoods, IL: Wolters Kluwer.

Hage, J., and C. Powers. 1992. *Post-industrial lives: Roles and relationships in the 21st century.* New York: Sage Publications, Inc.

Hales, C. 1999. Leading horses to water? The impact of decentralization on managerial behaviour. *Journal of Management Studies* 36 (November): 831–51.

Handy, C. 1997. Unimagined futures. In *The organization of the future*, ed. F. Hesselbein, M. Goldsmith, and R. Beckhard, 377–383. San Francisco: Jossey-Bass.

Handy, C. 1995. Trust and the virtual organization. *Harvard Business Review* 73 (May/June): 40–7.

Hobbs, B., and M. Aubry. 2008. An empirically grounded search for a typology of project management offices. *Project Management Journal* 39 (August): S69–S82.

Hurt, M., and J. Thomas. 2009. Building value through sustainable project management offices. *Project Management Journal* 40 (March): 55–72.

Karl, K. 1999. Mastering virtual teams book review. *The Academy of Management Executive* 13 (August): 118–119.

Kelley, E. 2001. Keys to effective virtual global teams. *Academy of Management Executive* 15.2: 132.

Kerzner, H. 2009. *Project management: A systems approach to planning, scheduling, and controlling.* 10th ed. Hoboken, NJ: John Wiley & Sons, Inc.

Kezsbom, D. 2000. Creating teamwork in virtual teams. *Publication of the American Association of Cost Engineers* 42 (October): 30–33.

King, A. S. 1997. The crescendo effect in career motivation. *Career Development International* 2.6: 293–301.

Krajewski, L., and L. Ritzman. 1996. *Operations management, strategy and analysis.* 4th ed. Reading, MA: Addison-Wesley Publishing Company.

Lai, Y., and B. Burchell. 2008. Distributed work: Communication in an "officeless firm." *New Technology, Work and Employment* 23 (March/April): 61–76.

Lipnack, J., and J. Stamps. 1997. *Virtual teams: Reaching across space, time, and organizations with technology.* New York: John Wiley & Sons, Inc.

Mayer, M. 2010. *The virtual edge: Embracing technology for distributed project team success.* 2nd ed. Newtown Square, PA: Project Management Institute.

Majchrzak, A., A. Malhotra, J. Stamps, and J. Lipnack. 2004. Can absence make a team grow stronger? *Harvard Business Review* 82.5: 131.

Maznevski, M., and K. Chudoba. 2000. Bridging space over time: Global virtual team dynamics and effectiveness. *Organization Science: A Journal of the Institute of Management Sciences* 11.5: 473.

Milosevic, D., L. Inman, and A. Ozbay. 2001. Impact of project management standardization on project effectiveness. *Engineering Management Journal* 13.4 (December): 9–16.

Morgan, G. 1998. *Images of organization.* Thousand Oaks, CA: Sage Publications.

O'Connor, C. 2000. Building the virtual team. *Accountancy Ireland* 32 (August): 20–21.

Ormand, J., J. Bruner, L. Birkemo, J. Hinderliter-Smith, and J. Veitch. 2000. A centralized global automation group in a decentralized organization. *Journal of Automated Methods and Management Chemistry* 22 (November): 195–198.

Project Management Institute. 2008. *A guide to the project management body of knowledge (PMBOK® guide).* 4th ed. Newtown Square, PA: Project Management Institute.

Roberts, K., E. Kossek, and C. Ozeki. 1998. Managing the global workforce: Challenges and strategies. *Academy of Management Executive* 12.4: 93.

Runyon, J. M. 2010. Faculty mentoring and student engagement are keys to success in the virtual classroom. *Community College Week* (Spring).

Schein, E. H. 2004. *Organizational culture and leadership.* 3rd ed. San Francisco: Jossey-Bass.

Schein, E. H. 1992. *Organizational culture and leadership.* 2nd ed. San Francisco: Jossey-Bass.

Scholz, C. 1998. *Towards the virtual corporation: A complex move along three axes.* http://www.orga.uni-sb.de./bibliothek/nr62.pdf.

Smith, A. 1904. *The Wealth of Nations.* London: Methuen and Co.

Spector, R., and P. McCarthy. 2005. *The Nordstrom way to customer service excellence: A handbook for implementing great service in your organization.* Hoboken, NJ: John Wiley & Sons, Inc.

Toney, F. 2002. *The superior project organization: Global competency standards and best practices.* New York: Marcel Dekker.

Townsend, A., and S. DeMarie. 1998. Keys to effective virtual global teams. *Academy of Management Executive* 12.3: 17.

Webster, J., and W. K. P. Wong. 2008. Comparing traditional and virtual group forms: Identity, communication, and trust in naturally occurring project teams. *The International Journal of Human Resource Management* 19 (January): 41–62.

Whymark, K., and S. Ellis. 1999. Whose career is it anyway? Options for career management in flatter organization structures. *Career Development International* 4.2.

World-Check. 2011. *Foreign Corrupt Practices Act.* http://www.fcpa.us.

Additional Resources

Beranek, P., J. Broder, B. Reining, N. Romano, and S. Sump. 2005. Management of virtual project teams: Guidelines for team leaders. *Communications of the Association for Information Systems* 16: 247–259.

Department for Business Innovation and Skills. 2010. Case study: Running a successful programme management office, POSTCOMM. http://www.bis.gov.uk/assets/biscore/corporate/docs/r/running-a-successful-pmo-postcomm.pdf.

Gorelick, C. K. 2000. Toward an understanding of organizational learning and collaborative technology: A case study of structuration and sensemaking in a virtual project team. *Dissertation Abstracts International* 61: 1806A. (UMI No. 9973090)

Johnson, D., and F. Johnson. 2000. *Joining together: Group theory and group skills.* Needham Heights, MA: Pearson.

Joy-Matthews, J., and B. Gladstone. 2000. Extending the group: A strategy for virtual team formation. *Industrial and Commercial Training* 32 (January): 24–29.

Marek, K. 2009. Learning to teach online: Creating a culture of support for faculty. *Journal of Education for Library and Information Science* 50.4. http://jelis.org/featured/learning-to-teach-online-creating-a-culture-of-support-for-faculty-by-kate-marek/.

MBA Knowledge Base. 2010. *Case study: Project management improves Lenovo's strategy execution and core competitiveness.* http://www.mbaknol.com/management-case-studies/case-study-project-management-improves-lenovos-strategy-execution-and-core-competitiveness/.

Mitchell, R. L. G. 2009. Online education and organizational change. *Community College Review* 37 (July).

Planview. 2009. *ESPN offers winning strategy for improved project management.* http://mareshcommunications.com/sitebuildercontent/sitebuilderfiles/planview-case-study-espn.pdf.

Project Management Institute. 2008. *The standard for program management.* 2nd ed. Newtown Square, PA: Project Management Institute.

INDEX

The Project Management Answer Book
Jeff Furman, PMP

In a highly accessible question-and-answer format, *The Project Management Answer Book* is a ready resource for everyone involved in project management. The book covers all aspects of project management, highlighting best practices and real-world tips and techniques, all in sync with PMI's *A Guide to the Project Management Body of Knowledge* (*PMBOK® Guide*). **Bonus!** Networking and social media tips for project managers, as well as formulas, tips, and a quick study sheet for preparing for the PMP® certification exam.
ISBN 978-1-56726-297-1 ■ Product Code B971 ■ 416 pages

Guerrilla Project Management
Kenneth T. Hanley, M. Eng. (Project Management)

To manage effectively in today's complex project environment, you need a framework of project management (PM) competencies, processes, and tools that can be put to use immediately and that flexes and scales to meet the needs of any project. In *Guerrilla Project Management,* Ken Hanley emphasizes key project management competencies, including managing stakeholders effectively, assessing risk accurately, and getting agreement on the objective measures of project success. Focusing on these and other competencies as well as effective PM processes and tools, Hanley presents an alternative approach to project management that is light, fast, and flexible—and adapts readily to the many changes every project manager faces. This is *the* go-to guide for today's nimble project manager!
ISBN 978-1-56726-294-0 ■ Product Code B940 ■ 236 pages

Integrated Cost and Schedule Control in Project Management, Second Edition
Ursula Kuehn, PMP

Building on the solid foundation of the first edition, this updated second edition includes new material on project planning in the federal government, integrated baseline reviews (IBRs), federal requirements for an ANSI/EIA-748 compliant earned value management system, and federal requirements for contract performance reports (CPRs). *Integrated Cost and Schedule Control in Project Management, Second Edition,* continues to offer a practical approach that is accessible to project managers at all levels. The step-by-step presentation, numerous case studies, and instructive examples give practitioners relevant material they can put to use immediately.
ISBN 978-1-56726-296-4 ■ Product Code B964 ■ 319 pages

Project Team Dynamics: Enhancing Performance, Improving Results
Lisa DiTullio

Companies that embrace the power of collaboration realize that the best way to solve complex problems is to build cohesive teams made up of members with different skills and expertise. Getting teams to work productively is at the heart of project management. Developing the structure for teams to work at a high level of efficiency and effectiveness is at the heart of this book. Lisa DiTullio clearly outlines methods for creating and implementing a framework to deal with the inevitable difficulties that any team will encounter. With examples drawn from contemporary project management, she demonstrates the effectiveness of this straightforward approach and the risks of not building a strong team culture.
ISBN 978-1-56726-290-2 ■ Product Code B902 ■ 179 pages